Harvard Business Review

ON

CORPORATE ETHICS

THE HARVARD BUSINESS REVIEW
PAPERBACK SERIES

The series is designed to bring today's managers and professionals the fundamental information they need to stay competitive in a fast-moving world. From the preeminent thinkers whose work has defined an entire field to the rising stars who will redefine the way we think about business, here are the leading minds and landmark ideas that have established the *Harvard Business Review* as required reading for ambitious businesspeople in organizations around the globe.

Other books in the series:

Harvard Business Review Interviews with CEOs

Harvard Business Review on Advances in Strategy

Harvard Business Review on Becoming a High Performance Manager

Harvard Business Review on Brand Management

Harvard Business Review on Breakthrough Leadership

Harvard Business Review on Breakthrough Thinking

Harvard Business Review on Building Personal and Organizational Resilience

Harvard Business Review on Business and the Environment

Harvard Business Review on the Business Value of IT

Harvard Business Review on Change

Harvard Business Review on Compensation

Harvard Business Review on Corporate Governance

Harvard Business Review on Corporate Responsibility

Harvard Business Review on Corporate Strategy

Harvard Business Review on Crisis Management

Harvard Business Review on Culture and Change

Harvard Business Review on Customer Relationship Management

Harvard Business Review on Decision Making

Harvard
Business
Review

ON
CORPORATE ETHICS

A HARVARD BUSINESS REVIEW PAPERBACK

The *Harvard Business Review* articles in this collection are available as individual reprints. Discounts apply to quantity purchases. For information and ordering, please contact Customer Service, Harvard Business School Publishing, Boston, MA 02163. Telephone: (617) 783-7500 or (800) 988-0886, 8 A.M. to 6 P.M. Eastern Time, Monday through Friday. Fax: (617) 783-7555, 24 hours a day. E-mail: custserv@hbsp.harvard.edu

Library of Congress Cataloging-in-Publication Data
Harvard business review on corporate ethics.
        p.   cm. — (The Harvard business review paperback series)
Includes index.
    ISBN 1-59139-273-X (alk. paper)
    1. Business ethics. 2. Social ethics. I. Title: Corporate ethics. II. Harvard business review. III. Series.
HF5387 .H3748 2003
174´.4—dc21   2003008216
                                                                              CIP

The paper used in this publication meets the requirements of the American National Standard for Permanence of Paper for Publications and Documents in Libraries and Archives Z39.48-1992.

Contents

Harvard Business Review

ON

CORPORATE ETHICS

We Don't Need Another Hero

JOSEPH L. BADARACCO, JR.

Executive Summary

EVERYBODY LOVES THE STORIES of heroes like Martin Luther King, Jr., Mother Teresa, and Gandhi. But the heroic model of moral leadership usually doesn't work in the corporate world. Modesty and restraint are largely responsible for the achievements of the most effective moral leaders in business.

The author, a specialist in business ethics, says the quiet leaders he has studied follow four basic rules in meeting ethical challenges and making decisions. The rules constitute an important resource for executives who want to encourage the development of such leaders among their middle managers.

The first rule is "Put things off till tomorrow." The passage of time allows turbulent waters to calm and lets leaders' moral instincts emerge. "Pick your battles" means that quiet leaders don't waste political capital on

1

fights they can't win; they save it for occasions when they really want to fight. "Bend the rules, don't break them" sounds easier than it is—bending the rules in order to resolve a complicated situation requires imagination, discipline, restraint, flexibility, and entrepreneurship. The fourth rule, "Find a compromise," reflects the author's finding that quiet leaders try not to see situations as polarized tests of ethical principles. These individuals work hard to craft compromises that are "good enough"— responsible and workable enough—to satisfy themselves, their companies, and their customers.

The vast majority of difficult problems are solved through the consistent striving of people working far from the limelight. Their quiet approach to leadership doesn't inspire, thrill, or provide story lines for uplifting TV shows. But the unglamorous efforts of quiet leaders make a tremendous difference every day in the corporate world.

E VERYBODY LOVES THE STORIES of great leaders, especially great moral leaders. Think of Martin Luther King, Jr., Mother Teresa, and Gandhi. We exalt these individuals as role models and celebrate their achievements. They represent, we proclaim, the gold standard of ethical behavior.

Or do they? I don't ask this because I question the value of ethical behavior—far from it. I ask because over the course of my career as a specialist in business ethics, I have observed that the most effective moral leaders in the corporate world often sever the connection between morality and public heroism. These men and women aren't high-profile champions of right over wrong and don't want to be. They don't spearhead large-scale ethical crusades. They move patiently, carefully, and incrementally. They right—or prevent—moral wrongs in the workplace inconspicuously and usually without casualties. I have come to call these people quiet leaders because their modesty and restraint are in large measure responsible for their extraordinary achievements. And since many big problems can only be resolved by a long series of small efforts, quiet leadership, despite its seemingly slow pace, often turns out to be the quickest way to make the corporation—and the world—a better place.

In this article, I explore the findings of my four-year effort to understand how quiet leaders see themselves, think about ethical problems, and make effective decisions. Although all names have been changed, the anecdotes below are based on more than 150 case studies that I gathered from several sources, including direct observation, participation in situations as an adviser, and papers and accounts by many of my older MBA students who came from corporate positions with serious management responsibilities. The stories have convinced me that while certain ethical challenges require direct, public action, quiet leadership is the best way to do the right thing in many cases. That's because quiet leadership is practical, effective, and sustainable. Quiet leaders prefer to pick their battles and fight them carefully rather than go down in a blaze of glory for a single, dramatic effort.

Two Ethical Approaches

To understand why quiet moral leadership works so well, consider what can result from a public display of heroism. Rebecca Waide was a manager at a small regional bank. Convinced that a set of lending policies was exploitative, she made an appointment with her boss and quickly launched into a made-for-Hollywood speech about the rights of the poor. "I can almost swear that while I was talking, there was inspirational music in the background," she says. "I must have sounded like Sally Field in *Norma Rae*. I wanted to defend the oppressed."

It didn't work. Waide's emotionalism and lack of careful preparation undermined her credibility. The company thought its policies were sound, particularly for riskier customers, and her boss didn't appreciate the lecture. Not surprisingly, the company's lending policies remained unchanged.

Now consider Barry Nelan, another banker whose case I studied. He was going through files one day when he discovered that a company had been charged too little interest on a bank loan for more than five years. He wondered if the bank's executives, some of whom were good friends with the borrower's managers, knew about the problem but were conveniently overlooking it. He feared that his boss, who had authorized the loan, might be scapegoated if the problem came to the attention of others.

At first, Nelan saw only two choices. He could report the error through official channels and let the chips fall where they might, or he could leave things alone. But then he came up with an alternative: He took the matter directly to his boss. His boss's first instinct was to rebury the problem, but Nelan said that if they couldn't find an answer, he would be forced to inform bank executives about the mistake. They sat down with the client and restructured the loan, then reported the problem and the solution to the executives. Nelan was careful, patient, and politically astute throughout the process. He managed to benefit himself and the organization while protecting his colleague's job. He was the quintessential quiet leader.

Operating Instructions

My research suggests that quiet moral leaders follow four basic rules in meeting ethical challenges and making decisions. Although not always used together, the rules constitute an indispensable tool kit that can help quiet leaders work out the dilemmas they face. Some tactics may seem a little too clever or even ethically dubious. Certainly, few people would want to work at jobs where such moves constitute business as usual. Nevertheless, these guidelines often prove critical when leaders have real responsibilities to meet.

The rules serve another purpose, too. By offering insight into how an organization's unknown soldiers achieve their moral victories, the guidelines can help top executives foster the development of quiet leaders among middle managers. Tactics they can use include setting examples of quiet leadership in meetings; going out of the way to praise and reward individuals who take quiet, sustained, effective approaches to problems; and appointing top managers who are themselves quiet leaders. Such actions send powerful messages about the right way to deal with difficult, messy problems.

PUT THINGS OFF TILL TOMORROW

When ethical dilemmas heat up, quiet leaders often look for ways to buy time. Careful execution of this tactic can spell the difference between success and failure. The passage of time allows turbulent waters to calm. It also lets leaders analyze the subtle ways in which individuals and events interact—it lets them look for patterns and watch for opportunities to arise from the flow of events. More important, sound moral instincts have a chance to emerge. Of course, there are situations—such as when a

defective product is about to be shipped or a misleading
financial report is about to be released—that call for
immediate action. But the drama of do-or-die situations
can lead us to exaggerate the frequency with which they
arise. The vast majority of practical ethical challenges
facing most managers are mundane and subtle, calling
for the unglamorous virtues of patience and staying
power.

To see how quiet leaders create buffer zones that permit them to put their unglamorous virtues to use, let's
look at a quiet leader who succeeded in thinking clearly
and moving at a deliberate pace, even though top management was breathing down his neck. Kyle Williams
had recently become a branch president for a small
regional bank in Maine. He was excited about a job that
gave him visibility and profit-and-loss responsibility.
The only drawback to the promotion was the intense
financial pressure on the bank and its senior executives.
Williams was told that if the stock price didn't rise
quickly, the bank was likely to be bought and dismantled
by a larger bank.

Among the 55 employees Williams inherited were
four chronic underperformers, including a 56-year-old
teller who was notoriously rude to customers and raised
the issue of age discrimination whenever her performance was questioned. Another of the four was a widow
who had been at the bank 30 years. She was recovering
from cancer surgery but was reluctant to go on disability.
Finally, there were the two lead loan officers: One lacked
initiative and imagination; he did everything by the
book. The other had more potential, but even the promise of a performance bonus didn't fire her up.

Williams was eager to reduce expenses, but he wanted
to avoid shortsighted cost-cutting measures and to be
fair to longtime employees. He thought firing the four

underperformers, as was tacitly but clearly expected of him, might embroil the company in legal problems. He needed time to persuade his boss to take a different approach, such as transferring the underperformers or encouraging them to take early retirement. If there had been less stress on the bank, Williams would have openly argued for moving slowly. But given the pressures, a request for more time could have prompted the bank management to replace him with someone willing to clean house more quickly. So he took steps to divert attention while he postponed action. Call it game playing if you will, but Williams's games were hardly trivial amusements. They were tactics that allowed him to find a "good enough" solution to the bank's problems.

There are two kinds of time buying: quick fixes and strategic stalling. Everyday dodges such as, "I've got someone on the other line—can I get back to you on that?" can buy a few hours or a couple of days; such gambits have helped countless managers whose backs were against the wall. But Williams needed weeks to rectify the situation he inherited. His situation called for strategic stalling.

The fundamental line of attack in strategic stalling is to dot all the i's and cross all the t's. As a first step, Williams tossed his boss a bone by cutting a few unnecessary expenses (badly managed operations often have plenty of those). He then sought legal advice on his personnel issues—after all, one employee had already raised the issue

Before they take stands or tackle tough problems, quiet leaders calculate how much political capital they are putting at risk and what they can expect in return.

of age discrimination. He also got human resources involved, a move that gained him weeks. Then he began to raise strategic questions: Do we have the appropriate contingency plans in place? Are there more options we should evaluate?

Strategic stalling gave Williams time to resolve all the issues he faced. He never caught the teller being rude, but he fired her for leaving large amounts of cash unattended. The widow went on permanent disability. After pep talks, quotas, and incentives failed to motivate the two loan officers, Williams threatened to fire them. One quit; the other, galvanized into action, became a first-rate loan officer.

PICK YOUR BATTLES

Political capital is the hard currency of organizational life. You earn it by establishing a reputation for getting things done and by having a network of people who can appreciate and reward your efforts. Political capital is hard to accumulate and devilishly easy to dissipate. That's why quiet leaders invest it astutely and use it with care. Before they take stands or tackle tough problems, quiet leaders calculate how much political capital they are putting at risk and what they can expect in return. In other words, they pick their battles wisely.

For an example of how not to squander political capital, consider Michele Petryni, the public relations manager at a large Washington, DC, law firm. Petryni stood in astonishment one day as she was refused admittance to a meeting with several law partners. The purpose of the meeting was to deal with a very sensitive problem in the firm, and for several weeks Petryni had been working with one of the partners on a solution. Now the partner was telling her that a "nonpartner female" would stir up the brew.

Petryni was shocked and furious. Her first impulse was to threaten a discrimination lawsuit. But Petryni was also shrewd. She understood that most of the time, getting on a white horse and leading a charge does little good. If she forced her way into the meeting, no one would be openly sympathetic and a few partners would be overtly hostile. Besides, she liked her job. She had been promoted rapidly and was widely respected in the firm. She didn't want to be labeled a troublemaker. So Petryni decided not to waste her hard-earned political capital. She opted for pointed humor instead.

"You know," she said to the partner she had been working with, "I've never been told I couldn't play ball because I didn't have the right equipment!" He appreciated her effort to smooth over the rupture and later told the senior partner what happened. The senior partner sought

Instead of acting like moral bookkeepers, quiet leaders bend the rules and own up to their deeper responsibilities.

out Petryni and apologized for the firm. He acknowledged there were sexists in the firm but said they were an aging minority. He asked Petryni for her patience and support.

How well did Petryni handle this situation? Her tactics didn't fit the standard model of heroic leadership. She didn't tell the first partner that he was doing something obnoxious, insulting, and perhaps illegal. She didn't go to the meeting, even though she belonged there. Many people would argue that she surrendered her interests. But Petryni made a prudent investment. Her restrained approach enabled her to make her case to the partner she had worked with and the senior partner without offending either. Of course, her efforts didn't change the firm's culture, but she was able to get management to acknowledge that there was a problem. Most important, Petryni added untold riches to her political capital for the occasions when she really wants to fight.

BEND THE RULES, DON'T BREAK THEM

Most of us don't associate bending the rules with moral leadership. But following the rules can be a moral cop-out. If a friend asks if you like her new shoes, and you think they look ridiculous, you don't tell the truth. And when the Gestapo demanded to know who was hiding Jews, some people lied. Between the trivial and the tragic are many everyday situations in which responsible people work hard to find ways to maneuver within the boundaries set by the rules. Instead of acting like moral bookkeepers, they bend the rules and own up to their deeper responsibilities.

Consider Jonathan Balint, a consultant who was working on a large project for a manufacturing company. Balint's brother-in-law happened to work for the client and was trying to decide whether to take an offer from another company or stay in his present job. Balint had learned that the client was three weeks away from announcing a major layoff; Balint's brother-in-law would likely lose his job. Should Balint tip him off to the danger of staying at the company?

Balint didn't want to betray the confidentiality of his client or his firm; doing so, he knew, would be wrong, and it could severely hurt his career. So he spent several days searching for wiggle room. He took the rules seriously but didn't treat them as a paint-by-numbers exercise. Eventually he decided he could send signals to his brother-in-law without revealing everything he knew.

For example, he reminded him that no one is indispensable, that anyone can be laid off; Balint also said he had heard rumors about impending layoffs at local manufacturers. His brother-in-law took the hint.

Balint's choice perfectly illustrates the way quiet leaders work. They know that breaking the rules is wrong—and in some cases illegal. They also want to protect their reputations, networks, and career prospects. So they don't break the rules. But when situations are complicated, they typically search for ways to bend the rules imaginatively. Quiet leaders don't view such tactics as ideal ways to handle problems, but sometimes situations give them no choice. Balint, for example, had competing obligations to his client and his family. In complex ethical situations such as these, bending the rules is never easy and certainly not fun. Indeed, bending the rules—as opposed to breaking them—is hard work. It requires imagination, discipline, and restraint, along with flexibility and entrepreneurship.

FIND A COMPROMISE

Compromise has a bad reputation in some circles. For some people, compromise is what politicians and lobbyists do in smoke-filled rooms. Many of us believe that good people—moral people—refuse to compromise. They tell the truth, the whole truth, and nothing but the truth, and they are always fair. Quiet leaders understand this view of moral principles, but they don't find it particularly useful in most situations. They reject the idea that moral principles can be treated like salami and sacrificed slice by slice, but they try not to see situations as black-and-white tests of ethical principles. For this reason, crafting responsible, workable compromises is not just something that quiet leaders occasionally do. It defines who they are.

Take Roger Darco, for example. Darco was a hardworking, successful sales rep who learned he wouldn't be able to sell a longtime customer a new server it needed. The servers were in limited supply, and his company was saving them for "premier" customers. Roger raised the issue with his boss and got lots of sympathy—but no assistance. Instead, his boss reminded him of the importance of making quota.

On the face of it, Darco had only two options. He could refuse to give his client the server, or he could violate company policy and sell the server by faking documents, as some reps were doing. But somewhere between extremes there is often a compromise solution. Darco found it by discovering that if his client was willing to be a test site, it could get the server early. The client agreed and got the machine it needed.

Darco may not look like much of a moral hero, but he did take on a complicated ethical issue and get it right. He didn't start a revolution—the situation didn't call for a revolution. Yet by finding a workable compromise, Darco uncovered a middle that was "good enough"— responsible enough and workable enough—to satisfy his customer, his company, and himself.

The Silence Between the Waves

The quiet approach to leadership is easy to misunderstand and mock. It doesn't inspire or thrill. It focuses on small things, careful moves, controlled and measured efforts. It doesn't provide story lines for uplifting TV shows. In contrast to heroic leadership, quiet leadership doesn't show us the heights that the human spirit can reach. What, then, do the imperfect, unglamorous, everyday efforts of quiet leaders amount to? Almost everything. The vast majority of difficult human problems are not solved by the dramatic efforts of people at the top but by the consistent striving of people working far from the limelight.

This was the view of Albert Schweitzer, a hero if ever there was one. After he won the 1952 Nobel Peace Prize for working with the poor in central Africa, Schweitzer used the money to build a facility for treating leprosy. He changed many lives and inspired countless others. Yet he was unromantic about the role of great moral heroes in shaping the world: "Of all the will toward the ideal in mankind only a small part can manifest itself in public action," he wrote. "All the rest of this force must be content with small and obscure deeds. The sum of these, however, is a thousand times stronger than the acts of those who receive wide public recognition. The latter, compared to the former, are like the foam on the waves of a deep ocean."

Ordinary People

THE QUIET MORAL LEADERS in my study typically work in the middle of organizations where they look for modest but effective solutions to the problems they face. They don't aspire to perfection. In fact, their thinking is distinguished by two characteristics that would almost certainly disqualify them for sainthood: Their motivations are decidedly mixed, and their worldviews are unabashedly realistic. Let's take a closer look at each of these traits.

Mixed Motives

According to the heroic model of moral leadership, true leaders make great sacrifices for the benefit of others. In truth, however, very few people would sacrifice their lives for a cause (which is why we revere the handful of people who do and why we call them saints and heroes). Most people, most of the time, act out of mixed and complex motives. They want to help others, but they also care about themselves. They have lives, interests, and commitments that they are unwilling to risk. Because they need to put food on the table, crusades and martyrdom are not options.

Consider John Ayer, an experienced sales rep at a major pharmaceutical company that had been selling physicians a very popular drug for treating depression. Although federal laws forbade it, the company started discreetly promoting the drug to doctors whose patients wanted to lose weight or stop smoking. Ayer didn't want to limit his pay or promotion prospects, but he didn't want to break the law or contribute to patients suffering side effects from unapproved uses. So he tried to walk a fine line: He talked about unapproved uses of the drug only if doctors asked him. But as more and more of his sales came from those uses, he became increasingly troubled and decided to stop answering questions about unapproved uses. He also visited doctors who were prescribing the drug for problems other than depression and discussed the risks and side effects with them. Then he went a step further: He told his manager and a few other sales reps what he was doing and why, in part to protect himself against future liability.

By any standard of moral purity, Ayer doesn't measure up very well. His motives for doing the right thing are unmistakably self-serving. As he puts it: "My decision was made as much out of fear as anything else. I was scared of finding out that a patient had died because one of my clients had prescribed the drug at a high dose. I also suspected that my company would not stand behind me if something horrible happened."

Although Ayer's motives were hardly unadulterated, they nonetheless gave him the strength to persevere. Indeed, when there is a tough moral challenge, the degree of a person's motivation can matter more than the purity of the motives. That's because real leaders draw strength from a multitude of motives—high and low, conscious and unconscious, altruistic and self-serving. The challenge is not to suppress self-interest or low motives but to harness, channel, and direct them. If Ayer had been motivated by empathy alone, I believe he would have been far less likely to act.

Of course, mixed motives can leave people in Ayer's position feeling bewildered and frustrated, but that's not all bad. Confusion in complex situations can prompt people to pause, look around, reflect, and learn before they plunge into action. Soldiers who clear minefields move slowly and methodically, but their deliberate pace takes nothing away from their valor and adds greatly to their effectiveness. Indeed, my research shows that when quiet leaders succeed, it is usually *because* of their complicated and ambivalent motives, not despite them.

Clinging to Reality

Ayer's quiet approach to leadership raises important questions. Should he have done more? Should he have taken the issue to senior management? Should he have blown the whistle and alerted federal regulators?

I believe the answer is no. All too often, whistle-blowing is career suicide. Torpedoing your career might be fine if you end up changing your company—or the world—for the better. But dramatic action seldom leads to such impressive results. Quiet leaders pay close attention to the limits of their power. They don't overestimate how much influence they have over other people or how well they can control events in an uncertain world. Each quiet leader realizes that, in most situations, he or she is only one piece on a chessboard.

Such realism is often confused with cynicism. But realists aren't cynics; they merely see things in Technicolor, whereas cynics see black and white. Quiet leaders' expansive vision of reality in all its colors helps them avoid acts of heroic self-immolation.

Consider Ben Waterhouse, the head of marketing at a medium-sized company. His boss asked him to drop a high-performing ad firm and replace it with a six-month-old agency. Waterhouse was flabbergasted, especially when he discovered that the owner of the new agency was a good friend of his boss. Waterhouse's immediate instinct was to dash off a strong memo or call a meeting with his boss's superior. But after he calmed down, Waterhouse recognized that he didn't have the clout to override his boss on this issue. So he developed a pragmatic plan. He gave the new ad agency a couple of very challenging assignments, which they handled poorly. He documented the failures to his boss, who opted to stick with the veteran agency.

From the perspective of heroism, Waterhouse's story seems more like a cop-out than a profile in courage. He didn't take a stand on principle; in fact, he engaged in subterfuge. But Waterhouse's realism was not a moral handicap—far from it. It gave him a sense of proportion and a degree of modesty and caution that helped him move wisely across a hazardous landscape. In the process, he managed to preserve one of the company's most valued relationships. He also kept his company from incurring unnecessary expenses. This made much more sense—realistically and ethically—than flaming out in a single heroic, but futile, act.

TAKEN TOGETHER, THE TRAITS OF mixed motives and hard-boiled realism describe the working assumptions of quiet moral leaders. A moral compass points these individuals in the right direction, but the guidelines for quiet leadership help them get to their destinations—in one piece.

Originally published in September 2001
Reprint R0108H

Ethics Without the Sermon

LAURA L. NASH

Executive Summary

"LIKE SOME TRIASSIC REPTILE, the theoretical view of
ethics lumbers along in the far past of Sunday School
and Philosophy I, while the reality of practical business
concerns is constantly measuring a wide range of competing claims on time and resources against the unrelenting and objective marketplace." So writes the author of
this article as she introduces a procedure to test pragmat-
ically the ethical content and human fallout of everyday
decisions in business and other organizational settings.
First you have to define the problem as you see it, then
(insofar as possible) examine it as outsiders might see it.
You explore where your loyalties lie and consider both
your intentions in making the decision and whom your
action might affect. You proceed to the consequences of
disclosing your action to those you report to or respect,
and then analyze the symbolic meaning to all affected.

19

In her conclusion the author attacks the sticky question of the proper moral standpoint of the organization as a whole.

A s IF VIA A NETWORK TV program on the telecommunications satellite, declarations such as these are being broadcast throughout the land.

Scene 1. Annual meeting, Anyproducts Inc.; John Q. Moneypockets, chairman and CEO, speaking: "Our responsibility to the public has always come first at our company, and we continue to strive toward serving our public in the best way possible in the belief that good ethics is good business. . . . Despite our forecast of a continued recession in the industry through 1982, we are pleased to announce that 1981's earnings per share were up for the twenty-sixth year in a row."

Scene 2. Corporate headquarters, Anyproducts Inc.; Linda Diesinker, group vice president, speaking: "Of course we're concerned about minority development and the plight of the inner cities. But the best place for our new plant would be Horsepasture, Minnesota. We need a lot of space for our operations and a skilled labor force, and the demographics and tax incentives in Horsepasture are perfect."

Scene 3. Interview with a financial writer; Rafe Short-stop, president, Anyproducts Inc., speaking: "We're very concerned about the state of American business and our ability to compete with foreign companies. . . . No, I don't think we have any real ethical problems. We don't bribe people or anything like that."

Scene 4. Jud McFisticuff, taxi driver, speaking: "Anyproducts? You've got to be kidding! I wouldn't buy their stuff for anything. The last thing of theirs I bought fell apart in six months. And did you see how they were dumping wastes in the Roxburg water system?"

Scene 5. Leslie Matriculant, MBA '82, speaking: "Join Anyproducts? I don't want to risk my reputation working for a company like that. They recently acquired a business that turned out to have ten class-action discrimination suits against it. And when Anyproducts tried to settle the whole thing out of court, the president had his picture in *Business Week* with the caption, 'His secretary still serves him coffee'."

Whether you regard it as an unchecked epidemic or as the first blast of Gabriel's horn, the trend toward focusing on the social impact of the corporation is an inescapable reality that must be factored into today's managerial decision making. But for the executive who asks, "How do we as a corporation examine our ethical concerns?" the theoretical insights currently available may be more frustrating than helpful.

As the first scene in this article implies, many executives firmly believe that corporate operations and corporate values are dynamically intertwined. For the purposes of analysis, however, the executive needs to uncoil the business-ethics helix and examine both strands closely.

Unfortunately, the ethics strand has remained largely inaccessible, for business has not yet developed a workable process by which corporate values can be articulated. If ethics and business are part of the same double helix, perhaps we can develop a microscope capable of enlarging our perception of both aspects of business administration—what we do and who we are.

Sidestepping Triassic Reptiles

Philosophy has been sorting out issues of fairness, injury, empathy, self-sacrifice, and so on for more than 2,000 years. In seeking to examine the ethics of business, therefore, business logically assumes it will be best served by a "consultant" in philosophy who is already familiar with the formal discipline of ethics.

As the philosopher begins to speak, however, a difficulty immediately arises; corporate executives and philosophers approach problems in radically different ways. The academician ponders the intangible, savors the paradoxical, and embraces the peculiar; he or she speaks in a special language of categorical imperatives and deontological view-points that must be taken into consideration before a statement about honesty is agreed to have any meaning.

Like some Triassic reptile, the theoretical view of ethics lumbers along in the far past of Sunday School and Philosophy I, while the reality of practical business concerns is constantly measuring a wide range of competing claims on time and resources against the unrelenting and objective marketplace.

Not surprisingly, the two groups are somewhat hostile. The jokes of the liberal intelligentsia are rampant and weary: *"Ethics and Business*—the shortest book in the world." "Business and ethics—a subject confined to the preface of business books." Accusations from the corporate cadre are delivered with an assurance that rests more on an intuition of social climate than on a certainty of fact: "You do-gooders are ruining America's ability to compete in the world." "Of course, the cancer reports on ____[choose from a long list] were terribly exaggerated." What is needed is a process of ethical inquiry that is immediately comprehensible to a group of executives and not predisposed to the utopian, and sometimes anti-capitalistic, bias marking much of the work in applied business philosophy today. So I suggest, as a preliminary solution, a set of 12 questions that draw on traditional philosophical frameworks but that avoid the level of abstraction normally associated with formal moral reasoning.

I offer the questions as a first step in a very new discipline. As such, they forma tentative model that will certainly undergo modifications after its parts are given some exercise. "Twelve Questions for Examining the Ethics of a Business Decision" poses the 12 questions.

To illustrate the application of the questions, I will draw especially on a program at Lex Service Group, Ltd., whose top management prepared a statement of financial objectives and moral values as a part of its strategic planning process.[1] Lex is a British company with operations in the United Kingdom and the United States. Its sales total about $1.2 billion. In 1978 its structure was partially decentralized, and in 1979 the chairman's policy group began a strategic planning process. The intent, according to its statement of values and objectives, was "to make explicit the sort of company Lex was, or wished to be."

Neither a paralegal code nor a generalized philosophy, the statement consisted of a series of general policies regarding financial strategy as well as such aspects of the company's character as customer service, employee-shareholder responsibility, and quality of management. Its content largely reflected the personal values of Lex's chairman and CEO, Trevor Chinn, whose private philanthropy is well known and whose concern for social welfare has long been echoed in the company's personnel policies.

In the past, pressure on senior managers for high profit performance had obscured some of these ideals in practice, and the statement of strategy was a way of radically realigning various competing moral claims with the financial objectives of the company. As one senior man-

---

Twelve Questions for Examining the Ethics of a Business Decision

1	Have you defined the problem accurately?
2	How would you define the problem if you stood on the other side of the fence?
3	How did this situation occur in the first place?
4	To whom and to what do you give your loyalty as a person and a member of the corporation?
5	What is your intention in making this decision?
6	How does this intention compare with the probable results?
7	Whom could your decision or action injure?
8	Can you discuss the problem with the affected parties before you make your decision?
9	Are you confident that your position will be as valid over a long period of time as it seems now?
10	Could you disclose without qualm your decision or action to your boss, your CEO, the board of directors, your family, society as a whole?
11	What is the symbolic potential of your action if understood? if misunderstood?
12	Under what conditions would you allow exceptions to your stand?

ager remarked to me, "The values seem obvious, and if we hadn't been so gross in the past we wouldn't have needed the statement." Despite a predictable variance among Lex's top executives as to the desirability of the values outlined in the statement, it was adopted with general agreement to comply and was scheduled for reassessment at a senior managers' meeting one year after implementation.

The 12 Questions

1 Have you defined the problem accurately?

How one assembles the facts weights an issue before the moral examination ever begins, and a definition is rarely accurate if it articulates one's loyalties rather than the facts. The importance of factual neutrality is readily seen, for example, in assessing the moral implications of producing a chemical agent for use in warfare. Depending on one's loyalties, the decision to make the substance can be described as serving one's country, developing products, or killing babies. All of the above may be factual statements, but none is neutral or accurate if viewed in isolation.

Similarly, the recent controversy over marketing U.S.-made cigarettes in Third World countries rarely noted that the incidence of lung cancer in underdeveloped nations is quite low (from one-tenth to one-twentieth the rate for U.S. males) due primarily to the lower life expectancies and earlier predominance of other diseases in these nations. Such a fact does not decide the ethical complexities of this marketing problem, but it does add a crucial perspective in the assignment of moral priorities by defining precisely the injury that tobacco exports may cause.

Extensive fact gathering may also help defuse the emotionalism of an issue. For instance, local statistics on lung cancer incidence reveal that the U.S. tobacco industry is not now "exporting death," as has been charged. Moreover, the substantial and immediate economic benefits attached to tobacco may be providing food and health care in these countries. Nevertheless, as life expectancy and the standards of living rise, a higher incidence of cigarette-related diseases appears likely to develop in these nations. Therefore, cultivation of the nicotine habit may be deemed detrimental to the long-term welfare of these nations.

According to one supposedly infallible truth of modernism, technology is so complex that its results will never be fully comprehensible or predictable. Part of the executive's frustration in responding to question 1 is the real possibility that the "experts" will find no grounds for agreement about the facts.

As a first step, however, defining fully the factual implications of a decision determines to a large degree the quality of one's subsequent moral position. Pericles' definition of true courage rejected the Spartans' blind obedience in war in preference to the courage of the Athenian citizen who, he said, was able to make a decision to proceed in full knowledge of the probable danger. A truly moral decision is an informed decision. A decision that is based on blind or convenient ignorance is hardly defensible.

One simple test of the initial definition is the question:

2 How would you define the problem if you stood on the other side of the fence?

The contemplated construction of a plant for Division X is touted at the finance committee meeting as an absolute necessity for expansion at a cost saving of at least 25%. With plans drawn up for an energy-efficient building and an option already secured on 99-year lease in a new industrial park in Chippewa County, the committee is likely to feel comfortable in approving the request for funds in a matter of minutes.

The facts of the matter are that the company will expand in an appropriate market, allocate its resources sensibly, create new jobs, increase Chippewa County's tax base, and most likely increase its returns to the shareholders. To the residents of Chippewa County, however, the plant may mean the destruction of a customary recreation spot, the onset of severe traffic jams, and the erection of an architectural eyesore. These are also facts of the situation, and certainly more immediate to the county than utilitarian justifications of profit performance and rights of ownership from an impersonal corporation whose headquarters are 1,000 miles from Chippewa County and whose executives have plenty of acreage for their own recreation.

The purpose of articulating the other side, whose needs are understandably less proximate than operational considerations, is to allow some mechanism whereby calculations of self-interest (or even of a project's ultimate general beneficence) can be interrupted by a compelling empathy for those who might suffer immediate injury or mere annoyance as a result of a corporation's decisions. Such empathy is a necessary prerequisite for shouldering voluntarily some responsibility for the social consequences of corporate operations, and it may be the only solution to today's overly litigious and anarchic world.

There is a power in self-examination: with an exploration of the likely consequences of a proposal, taken from the viewpoint of those who do not immediately benefit, comes a discomfort or an embarrassment that rises in proportion to the degree of the likely injury and its articulation. Like Socrates as gadfly, who stung his fellow citizens into a critical examination of their conduct when they became complacent, the discomfort of the alternative definition is meant to prompt a disinclination to choose the expedient over the most responsible course of action.

Abstract generalities about the benefits of the profit motive and the free market system are, for some, legitimate and ultimate justifications, but when unadorned with alternative viewpoints, such arguments also tend to promote the complacency, carelessness, and impersonality that have characterized some of the more injurious actions of corporations. The advocates of these arguments are like the reformers in Nathaniel Hawthorne's short story "Hall of Fantasy" who "had got possession of some crystal fragment of truth, the brightness of which so dazzled them that they could see nothing else in the whole universe."

In the example of Division X's new plant, it was a simple matter to define the alternate facts; the process rested largely on an assumption that certain values were commonly shared (no one likes a traffic jam, landscaping pleases more than an unadorned building, and so forth). But the alternative definition often underscores an inherent disparity in values or language. To some, the employment of illegal aliens is a criminal act (fact #1); to others, it is a solution to the 60% unemployment rate of a neighboring country (fact #2). One country's bribe is another country's redistribution of sales commissions.

When there are cultural or linguistic disparities, it is easy to get the facts wrong or to invoke a pluralistic tolerance as an excuse to act in one's own self-interest: "That's the way they do things over there. Who are we to question their beliefs?" This kind of reasoning can be both factually inaccurate (many generalizations about bribery rest on hearsay and do not represent the complexities of a culture) and philosophically inconsistent (there are plenty of beliefs, such as those of the environmentalist, which the same generalizers do not hesitate to question).

3 How did this situation occur in the first place?

Lex Motor Company, a subsidiary of Lex Service Group Ltd., had been losing share at a 20% rate in declining market; and Depot B's performance was the worst of all. Two nearby Lex depots could easily absorb B's business, and closing it down seemed the only sound financial decision. Lex's chairman, Trevor Chinn, hesitated to approve the closure, however, on the grounds that putting 100 people out of work was not right when the corporation itself was not really jeopardized by B's existence. Moreover, seven department managers, who were all within five years of retirement and had had 25 or more years of service at Lex, were scheduled to be made redundant.

The values statement provided no automatic solution, for it placed value on both employees' security and shareholders' interest. Should they close Depot B? At first Chinn thought not: Why should the little guys suffer disproportionately when the company was not performing well? Why not close a more recently acquired business where employee service was not so large a factor? Or why not wait out the short term and reduce head count through natural attrition?

As important as deciding the ethics of the situation was the inquiry into its history. Indeed, the history gave a clue to solving the dilemma: Lex's traditional emphasis on employee security *and* high financial performance had led to a precipitate series of acquisitions and subsequent divestitures when the company had failed to meet its overall objectives. After each rationalization, the people serving the longest had been retained and placed at Depot B, so that by 1980 the facility had more managers than it needed and a very high proportion of long-service employees.

So the very factors that had created the performance problems were making the closure decision difficult, and the very solution that Lex was inclined to favor again would exacerbate the situation further!

In deciding the ethics of a situation it is important to distinguish the symptoms from the disease. Great profit pressures with no sensitivity to the cycles in a particular industry, for example, may force division managers to be ruthless with employees, to short-weight customers, or even to fiddle with cash flow reports in order to meet headquarters' performance criteria.

Dealing with the immediate case of lying, quality discrepancy, or strained labor relations—when the problem is finally discovered—is only a temporary solution. A full examination of how the situation occurred and what the traditional solutions have been may reveal a more serious discrepancy of values and pressures, and this will illuminate the real significance and ethics of the problem. It will also reveal recurring patterns of events that in isolation appear trivial but that as a whole point up a serious situation.

Such a mechanism is particularly important because very few executives are outright scoundrels. Rather, violations of corporate and social values usually occur inadvertently because no one recognizes that a problem exists until it becomes a crisis. This tendency toward initial trivialization seems to be the biggest ethical problem in business today. Articulating answers to my first three questions is a way of reversing that process.

4 To whom and what do you give your loyalties as a person and as a member of the corporation?

Every executive faces conflicts of loyalty. The most familiar occasions pit private conscience and sense of duty against corporate policy, but equally frequent are the situations in which one's close colleagues demand participation (tacit or explicit) in an operation or a decision that runs counter to company policy. To whom or what is the greater loyalty—to one's corporation? superior? family? society? self? race? sex?

The good news about conflicts of loyalty is that their identification is a workable way of smoking out the ethics of a situation and of discovering the absolute values inherent in it. As one executive in a discussion of a Harvard case study put it, "My corporate brain says this action is O.K., but my noncorporate brain keeps flashing these warning lights."

The bad news about conflicts of loyalty is that there are few automatic answers for placing priorities on them. "To thine own self be true" is a murky quagmire when the self takes on a variety of roles, as it does so often in this complex modern world.

Supposedly, today's young managers are giving more weight to individual than to corporate identity, and some older executives see this tendency as being ultimately subversive. At the same time, most of them believe individual integrity is essential to a company's reputation.

The U.S. securities industry, for example, is one of the most rigorous industries in America in its requirements of honesty and disclosure. Yet in the end, all its systematic precautions prove inadequate unless the people involved also have a strong sense of integrity that puts loyalty to these principles above personal gain.

A system, however, must permit the time and foster the motivation to allow personal integrity to surface in a particular situation. An examination of loyalties is one way to bring this about. Such an examination may strengthen reputations but also may result in blowing the whistle (freedom of thought carries with it the risk of revolution). But a sorting out of loyalties can also bridge the gulf between policy and implementation or among various interest groups whose affiliations may mask a common devotion to an aspect of a problem—a devotion on which consensus can be built.

How does one probe into one's own loyalties and their implications? A useful method is simply to play various roles out loud, to call on one's loyalty to family and community (for example) by asking, What will I say when my child asks me why I did that?" If the answer is "That's the way the world works," then your loyalties are clear and moral passivity inevitable. But if the question presents real problems, you have begun a demodulation of signals from your conscience that can only enhance corporate responsibility.

5 What is your intention in making this decision?

6 How does this intention compare with the likely results?

These two questions are asked together because their content often bears close resemblance and, by most calculations, both color the ethics of a situation.

Corporation Buglebloom decides to build a new plant in an underdeveloped minority-populated district where the city has been trying with little success to encourage industrial development. The media approve and Bugle- bloom adds another star to its good reputation. Is Bugle- bloom a civic leader and a supporter of minorities or a canny investor about to take advantage of the disadvan- taged? The possibilities of Buglebloom's intentions are endless and probably unfathomable to the public; Bugle- bloom may be both canny investor and friend of minor- ity groups.

I argue that despite their complexity and elusiveness, a company's intentions *do* matter. The "purity" of Bugle- bloom's motives (purely profit-seeking or purely altruis- tic) will have wide-reaching effects inside and outside the corporation—on attitudes toward minority employ- ees in other parts of the company, on the wages paid at the new plant, and on the number of other investors in the same area—that will legitimize a certain ethos in the corporation and the community.

Sociologist Max Weber called this an "ethics of atti- tude" and contrasted it with an "ethics of absolute ends." An ethics of attitude sets a standard to ensure a certain action. A firm policy at headquarters of not cheating cus- tomers, for example, may also deter salespeople from succumbing to a tendency to lie by omission or pur- chasers from continuing to patronize a high-priced sup- plier when the costs are automatically passed on in the selling price.

What about the ethics of result? Two years later, Buglebloom wishes it had never begun Project Minority Plant. Every good intention has been lost in the realities of doing business in an unfamiliar area, and Buglebloom now has dirty hands: some of those payoffs were abso- lutely unavoidable if the plant was to open, operations have been plagued with vandalism and language prob- lems, and local resentment at the industrialization of the neighborhood has risen as charges of discrimination have surfaced. No one seems to be benefiting from the project.

The goodness of intent pales somewhat before results that perpetrate great injury or simply do little good. Common sense demands that the "responsible" corporation try to align the two more closely, to identify the probable consequences and also the limitations of knowledge that might lead to more harm than good. Two things to remember in comparing intention and results are that knowledge of the future is always inadequate and that overconfidence often precedes a disastrous mistake.

These two precepts, cribbed from ancient Greece, may help the corporation keep the disparities between intent and result a fearsome reality to consider continuously. The next two questions explore two ways of reducing the moral risks of being wrong.

7 Whom could your decision or action injure?

The question presses whether injury is intentional or not. Given the limits of knowledge about a new product or policy, who and how many will come into contact with it? Could its inadequate disposal affect an entire community? two employees? yourself? How might your product be used if it happened to be acquired by a terrorist radical group or a terrorist military police force? Has your distribution system or disposal plan ensured against such injury? Could it ever?

If not, there may be a compelling moral justification for stopping production. In an integrated society where business and government share certain values, possible injury is an even more important consideration than potential benefit. In policymaking, a much likelier ground for agreement than benefit is avoidance of injury through those "universal nos"—such as no mass death, no totalitarianism, no hunger or malnutrition, no harm to children.

To exclude *at the outset* any policy or decision that might have such results is to reshape the way modern business examines its own morality. So often business formulates questions of injury only after the fact in the form of liability suits.

8 Can you engage the affected parties in a discussion of the problem before you make your decision?

If the calculus of injury is one way of responding to limitations of knowledge about the probable results of a particular business decision, the participation of affected parties is one of the best ways of informing that consideration. Civil rights groups often complain that corporations fail to invite participation from local leaders during the planning stages of community development projects and charitable programs. The corporate foundation that builds a tennis complex for disadvantaged youth is throwing away precious resources if most children in the neighborhood suffer from chronic malnutrition.

In the Lex depot closure case I have mentioned, senior executives agonized over whether the employees would choose redundancy over job transfer and which course would ultimately be more beneficial to them. The managers, however, did not consult the employees. There were more than 200 projected job transfers to another town. But all the affected employees, held by local ties and uneasy about possibly lower housing subsidies, refused relocation offers. Had the employees been allowed to participate in the redundancy discussions, the company might have wasted less time on relocation plans or might have uncovered and resolved the fears about relocating.

The issue of participation affects everyone. (How many executives feel that someone else should decide what is in *their* best interest?) And yet it is a principle often forgotten because of the pressure of time or the inconvenience of calling people together and facing predictably hostile questions.

9 *Are you confident that your position will be as valid over a long period of time as it seems now?*

As anyone knows who has had to consider long-range plans and short-term budgets simultaneously, a difference in time frame can change the meaning of a problem as much as spring and autumn change the colors of a tree. The ethical coloring of a business decision is no exception to this generational aspect of decision making. Time alters circumstances, and few corporate value systems are immune to shifts in financial status, external political pressure, and personnel. (One survey now places the average U.S CEO's tenure in office at five years.)

At Lex, for example, the humanitarianism of the statement of objectives and values depended on financial prosperity. The values did not fully anticipate the extent to which the U.K. economy would undergo a recession, and the resulting changes had to be examined, reconciled, and fought if the company's values were to have any meaning. At the Lex annual review, the managers asked themselves repeatedly whether hard times were the ultimate test of the statement or a clear indication that a corporation had to be able to "afford" ethical positions.

Ideally, a company's articulation of its values should anticipate changes of fortune. As the hearings for the passage of the Foreign Corrupt Practices Act of 1977 demonstrated, doing what you can get away with today may not be a secure moral standard, but short-term discomfort for long-term sainthood may require irrational courage or a rational reasoning system or, more likely, both. These 12 questions attempt to elicit a rational system. Courage, of course, depends on personal integrity.

Another aspect of the ethical time frame stretches beyond the boundaries of question 9 but deserves special attention, and that is the timing of the ethical inquiry. When and where will it be made?

We do not normally invoke moral principles in our everyday conduct. Some time ago the participants in a national business ethics conference had worked late into the night preparing the final case for the meeting, and they were very anxious the next morning to get the class under way. Just before the session began, however, someone suggested that they all donate a dollar apiece as a gratuity for the dining hall help at the institute.

Then just as everyone automatically reached into his or her pocket, another person questioned the direction of the gift. Why tip the person behind the counter but not the cook in the kitchen? Should the money be given to each person in proportion to salary or divided equally among all? The participants laughed uneasily—or groaned—as they thought of the diversion of precious time from the case. A decision had to be made.

With the sure instincts of efficient managers, the group chose to forgo further discussion of distributive justice and, yes, appoint a committee. The committee doled out the money without further group consideration, and no formal feedback on the donation was asked for or given.

The questions offered here do not solve the problem of making time for the inquiry. For suggestions about creating favorable conditions for examining corporate values, drawn from my field research, see the "Shared Conditions of Some Successful Ethical Inquiries" at the end of this article.

10 Could you disclose without qualm your decision or action to your boss, your CEO, the board of directors, your family, or society as a whole?

The old question, "Would you want your decision to appear on the front page of the *New York Times?*" still holds. A corporation may maintain that there's really no problem, but a survey of how many "trivial" actions it is reluctant to disclose might be interesting. Disclosure is a way of sounding those submarine depths of conscience and of searching out loyalties.

It is also a way of keeping a corporate character cohesive. The Lex group, for example, was once faced with a very sticky problem concerning a small but profitable site with unpleasant (though in no way illegal) working conditions, where two men with 30 years' service worked. I wrote up the case for a Lex senior managers' meeting on the promise to disguise it heavily because the executive who supervised the plant was convinced that, if the chairman and the personnel director knew the plant's true location, they would close it down immediately.

At the meeting, however, as everyone became involved in the discussion and the chairman himself showed sensitivity to the dilemma, the executive disclosed the location and spoke of his own feelings about the situation. The level of mutual confidence was apparent to all, and by other reports it was the most open discussion the group had ever had.

The meeting also fostered understanding of the company's values and their implementation. When the discussion finally flagged, the chairman spoke up. Basing his views on a full knowledge of the group's understanding of the problem, he set the company's priorities. "Jobs over fancy conditions, health over jobs," Chinn said, "but we always *must disclose.*" The group decided to keep the plant open, at least for the time being.

Disclosure does not, however, automatically bring universal sympathy. In the early 1970s, a large food store chain that repeatedly found itself embroiled in the United Farm Workers (UFW) disputes with the Teamsters over California grape and lettuce contracts took very seriously the moral implications of a decision whether to stop selling these products. The company endlessly researched the issues, talked to all sides, and made itself available to public representatives of various interest groups to explain its position and to hear out everyone else.

When the controversy started, the company decided to support the UFW boycott, but three years later top management reversed its position. Most of the people who wrote to the company or asked it to send representatives to their local UFW support meetings, however, continued to condemn the chain even after hearing its views, and the general public apparently never became aware of the company's side of the story.

11 *What is the symbolic potential of your action if understood? if misunderstood?*

Jones Inc., a diversified multinational corporation with assets of $5 billion, has a paper manufacturing operation that happens to be the only major industry in Stirville, and the factory has been polluting the river on which it is located. Local and national conservation groups have filed suit against Jones Inc. for past damages, and the company is defending itself. Meanwhile, the corporation has adopted plans for a new waste-efficient plant. The legal battle is extended and local resentment against Jones Inc. gets bitter.

As a settlement is being reached, Jones Inc. announces that, as a civic-minded gesture, it will make 400 acres of Stirville woodland it owns available to the residents for conservation and recreation purposes. Jones's intention is to offer a peace pipe to the people of Stirville, and the company sees the gift as a symbol of its own belief in conservation and a way of signaling that value to Stirville residents and national conservation groups. Should Jones Inc. give the land away? Is the symbolism significant?

If the symbolic value of the land is understood as Jones Inc. intends, the gift may patch up the company's relations with Stirville and stave off further disaffection with potential employees as the new plant is being built. It may also signal to employees throughout the corporation that Jones Inc. places a premium on conservation efforts and community relations.

If the symbolic value is misunderstood, however, or if completion of the plant is delayed and the old one has to be put back in use—or if another Jones operation is discovered to be polluting another community and becomes a target of the press—the gift could be interpreted as nothing more than a cheap effort to pay off the people of Stirville and hasten settlement of the lawsuit.

The Greek root of our word *symbol* means both signal and contract. A business decision—whether it is the use of an expense account or a corporate donation—has a symbolic value in signaling what is acceptable behavior within the corporate culture and in making a tacit contract with employees and the community about the rules of the game. How the symbol is actually perceived (or misperceived) is as important as how you intend it to be perceived.

12 *Under what conditions would you allow exceptions to your stand?*

If we accept the idea that every business decision has an important symbolic value and a contractual nature, then the need for consistency is obvious. At the same time, it is also important to ask under what conditions the rules of the game may be changed. What conflicting principles, circumstances, or time constraints would provide a morally acceptable basis for making an exception to one's normal institutional ethos? For instance, how does the cost of the strategy to develop managers from minority groups over the long term fit in with short-term hurdle rates? Also to be considered is what would mitigate a clear case of employee dishonesty.

Questions of consistency—if you would do X, would you also do Y?—are yet another way of eliciting the ethics of the company and of oneself, and can be a final test of the strength, idealism, or practicality of those values. A last example from the experience of Lex illustrates this point and gives temporary credence to the platitude that good ethics is good business. An article in the Sunday paper about a company that had run a series of racy ads, with pictures of half-dressed women and promises of free merchandise to promote the sale of a very mundane product, sparked an extended examination at Lex of its policies on corporate inducements.

One area of concern was holiday giving. What was the acceptable limit for a gift—a bottle of whiskey? a case? Did it matter only that the company did not *intend* the gift to be an inducement, or did the mere possibility of inducement taint the gift? Was the cut-off point absolute? The group could agree on no halfway point for allowing some gifts and not others, so a new value was added to the formal statement that prohibited the offering or receiving of inducements.

The next holiday season Chinn sent a letter to friends and colleagues who had received gifts of appreciation in the past. In it he explained that, as a result of Lex's concern with "the very complex area of business ethics," management had decided that the company would no longer send any gifts, nor would it be appropriate for its employees to receive any. Although the letter did not explain Lex's reasoning behind the decision, apparently there was a large untapped consensus about such gift giving: by return mail Chinn received at least 20 letters from directors, general managers, and chairmen of companies with which Lex had done business congratulating him for his decision, agreeing with the new policy, and thanking him for his holiday wishes. (For more information on making ethical inquiries, see "Shared Conditions of Some Successful Ethical Inquiries" at the end of this article.)

The 'Good Puppy' Theory

The 12 questions are a way to articulate an idea of the responsibilities involved and to lay them open for examination. Whether a decisive policy is also generated or not, there are compelling reasons for holding such discussions:

- The process facilitates talk as a group about a subject that has traditionally been reserved for the privacy of one's conscience. Moreover, for those whose consciences twitch but don't speak in full sentences, the questions help sort out their own perceptions of the problem and various ways of thinking about it.

- The process builds a cohesiveness of managerial character as points of consensus emerge and people from vastly different operations discover that they share common problems. It is one way of determining the values and goals of the company, and that is a key element in determining corporate strategy.

- It acts as an information resource. Senior managers learn about other parts of the company with which they may have little contact.

- It helps uncover ethical inconsistencies in the articulated values of the corporation or between these values and the financial strategy.

- It helps uncover sometimes dramatic differences between the values and the practicality of their implementation.

- It helps the CEO understand how the senior managers think, how they handle a problem, and how willing and able they are to deal with complexity. It reveals how they may be drawing on the private self to the enhancement of corporate activity.

- In drawing out the private self in connection with business and in exploring the significance of the corporation's activities, the process derives meaning from an environment that is often characterized as meaningless.

- It helps improve the nature and range of alternatives.

- It is cathartic.

The process is also reductive in that it limits the level of inquiry. For example, the 12 questions ask what injury might result from a decision and what good is intended, but they do not ask the meaning of *good* or whether the result is "just."

Socrates asked how a person could talk of pursuing the good before knowing what the good is; and the analysis he visualized entailed a lifelong process of learning and examination. Do the 12 short questions, with their explicit goal of simplifying the ethical examination, bastardize the Socratic ideal? To answer this, we must distinguish between personal philosophy and participation as a corporate member in the examination of a *corporate* ethos, for the 12 questions assume some difference between private and corporate "goodness."

This distinction is crucial to any evaluation of my suggested process for conducting an ethical inquiry and needs to be explained. What exactly do we expect of the "ethical," or "good," corporation? Three examples of goodness represent prevailing social opinions, from that of the moral philosopher to the strict Friedmaniac.

1. The most rigorous moral analogy to the good corporation would be the "good man." An abstract, philosophical ideal having highly moral connotations, the good man encompasses an intricate relation of abstractions such as Plato's four virtues (courage, godliness or philosophical wisdom, righteousness, and prudence). The activities of this kind of good corporation imply a heavy responsibility to collectively know the good and to resolve to achieve it.

2. Next, there is the purely amoral definition of good, as in a "good martini"—an amoral fulfillment of a largely inanimate and functional purpose. Under this

definition, corporate goodness would be best achieved by the unadorned accrual of profits with no regard for the social implications of the means whereby profits are made.

3. Halfway between these two views lies the good as in "good puppy"—here goodness consists primarily of the fulfillment of a social contract that centers on avoiding social injury. Moral capacity is perceived as present, but its potential is limited. A moral evaluation of the good puppy is possible but exists largely in concrete terms; we do not need to identify the puppy's intentions as utilitarian to understand and agree that its "ethical" fulfillment of the social contract consists of not soiling the carpet or biting the baby.

It seems to me that business ethics operates most appropriately for corporate man when it seeks to define and explore corporate morality at the level of the good puppy. The good corporation is expected to avoid perpetrating irretrievable social injury (and to assume the costs when it unintentionally does injury) while focusing on its purpose as a profit-making organization. Its moral capacity does not extend, however, to determining by itself what will improve the general social welfare.

The good puppy inquiry operates largely in concrete experience; just as the 12 questions impose a limit on our moral expectations, so too they impose a limit (welcome, to some) on our use of abstraction to get at the problem.

The situations for testing business morality remain complex. But by avoiding theoretical inquiry and limiting the expectations of corporate goodness to a few rules for social behavior that are based on common sense, we can develop an ethic that is appropriate to the language, ideology, and institutional dynamics of business decision making and consensus. This ethic can also offer managers a practical way of exploring those occasions when their corporate brains are getting warning flashes from their noncorporate brains.

Shared Conditions of Some Successful Ethical Inquiries

Fixed time frame

Understanding and identifying moral issues takes time and causes ferment, and the executive needs an uninterrupted block of time to ponder the problems.

Unconventional location

Religious groups, boards of directors, and professional associations have long recognized the value of the retreat as a way of stimulating fresh approaches to regular activities. If the group is going to transcend normal corporate hierarchies, it should hold the discussion on neutral territory so that all may participate with the same degree of freedom.

Resource person

The advantage of bringing in an outsider is not that he or she will impose some preconceived notion of right and wrong on management but that he will serve as a midwife for bringing the values already present in the institution out into the open. He can generate closer examination of the discrepancies between values and practice and draw on a wider knowledge of instances and intellectual frameworks than the group can. The resource person may also take the important role of arbitrator—to ensure that one person does not dominate the session with his or her own values and that the dialogue does not become impossibly emotional.

Participation of CEO

In most corporations the chief executive still commands an extra degree of authority for the intangible we call corporate culture, and the discussion needs the perspective of and legitimization by that authority if it is to have any seriousness of purpose and consequence. One of the most interesting experiments in examining corporate policy I have observed lacked the CEO's support, and within a year it died on the vine.

Credo

Articulating the corporation's values and objectives provides a reference point for group inquiry and implementation. Ethical codes, however, when drawn up by the legal department, do not always offer a realistic and full representation of management's beliefs. The most important ethical inquiry for management may be the very formulation of such a statement, for the *process* of articulation is as useful as the values agreed on.

Homegrown topics

In isolating an ethical issue, drawing on your own experience is important. Philosophical business ethics has tended to reflect national social controversies, which though relevant to the corporation may not always be as relevant—not to mention as easily resolved—as some internal issues that are shaping the character of the company to a much greater degree. Executives are also more likely to be informed on these issues.

Resolution

In all the programs I observed except one, there was a point at which the inquiry was slated to have some resolution: either a vote on the issue, the adoption of a new policy, a timetable for implementation, or the formulation of a specific statement of values. The one program observed that had no such decision-making structure was organized simply to gather information about the company's activities through extrahierarchical channels. Because the program had no tangible goals or clearly articulated results, its benefits were impossible to measure.

Notes

1. The process is modeled after ideas in Kenneth R. Andrews's book *The Concept of Corporate Strategy* (Homewood, Ill.: Richard D. Irwin, 1980, revised edition) and in Richard F. Vancil's article "Strategy Formulation in Complex Organizations," *Sloan Management Review*, Winter 1976, p. 4.

Originally published in November–December 1981
Reprint 81609

Why 'Good' Managers Make Bad Ethical Choices

SAUL W. GELLERMAN

Executive Summary

NEWSPAPERS OFTEN CARRY STORIES of corporate misconduct. For decades, Manville Corporation suppressed the danger of asbestos inhalation; E.F. Hutton pleaded guilty to 2,000 counts of mail and wire fraud. How can normally honest, intelligent, and compassionate managers act in ways that seem callous, duplicitous, dishonest, and wrongheaded?

The answer is generally found in human nature—in the way ambition and duty get distorted under pressure. The border between right and wrong shifts in convenient directions, or is even ignored, though the manager has no intention of ignoring it.

The author explores the numerous rationalizations that lead to unethical behavior. He offers practical suggestions to help ensure the preservation of ethical propriety: establish clear ethical guidelines for all employees; stress formally and regularly that loyalty to the company does not excuse acts that jeopardize its good name; teach managers, "When in doubt, don't"; have company watchdogs to sniff out possible misdeeds; raise the frequency and unpredictability of audits and spot checks; when you detect a trespass, make the punishment quick, meaningful, and public. Above all, listen to your own moral voice. Chances are it's there saying "don't."

How could top-level executives at the Manville Corporation have suppressed evidence for decades that proved that asbestos inhalation was killing their own employees?

What could have driven the managers of Continental Illinois Bank to pursue a course of action that threatened to bankrupt the institution, ruined its reputation, and cost thousands of innocent employees and investors their jobs and their savings?

Why did managers at E.F. Hutton find themselves pleading guilty to 2,000 counts of mail and wire fraud, accepting a fine of $2 million, and putting up an $8 million fund for restitution to the 400 banks that the company had systematically bilked?

How can we explain the misbehavior that took place in these organizations—or in any of the others, public and private, that litter our newspapers' front pages: workers at a defense contractor who accused their superiors of falsifying time cards; alleged bribes and kickbacks that honeycombed New York City government; a company that knowingly marketed an unsafe birth control device; the decision-making process that led to the space shuttle Challenger tragedy.

The stories are always slightly different; but they have a lot in common since they're full of the oldest questions in the world, questions of human behavior and human judgment applied in ordinary day-to-day situations. Reading them we have to ask how usually honest, intelligent, compassionate human beings could act in ways that are callous, dishonest, and wrongheaded.

In my view, the explanations go back to four rationalizations that people have relied on through the ages to justify questionable conduct: believing that the activity is not "really" illegal or immoral; that it is in the individual's or the corporation's best interest; that it will never be found out; or that because it helps the company the company will condone it. By looking at these rationalizations in light of these cases, we can develop some practical rules to more effectively control managers' actions that lead to trouble—control, but not eliminate. For the hard truth is that corporate misconduct, like the lowly cockroach, is a plague that we can suppress but never exterminate.

Three Cases

Amitai Etzioni, professor of sociology at George Washington University, recently concluded that in the last ten years, roughly two-thirds of America's 500 largest corporations have been involved, in varying degrees, in some form of illegal behavior. By taking a look at three corporate cases, we may be able to identify the roots of the kind of misconduct that not only ruins some people's lives, destroys institutions, and gives business as a whole a bad name but that also inflicts real and lasting harm on a large number of innocent people. The three cases that follow should be familiar. I present them here as examples of the types of problems that confront managers in all kinds of businesses daily.

MANVILLE CORPORATION

A few years ago, Manville (then Johns Manville) was solid enough to be included among the giants of American business. Today Manville is in the process of turning over 80% of its equity to a trust representing people who have sued or plan to sue it for liability in connection with one of its principal former products, asbestos. For all practical purposes, the entire company was brought down by questions of corporate ethics.

More than 40 years ago, information began to reach Johns Manville's medical department—and through it, the company's top executives—implicating asbestos inhalation as a cause of asbestosis, a debilitating lung disease, as well as lung cancer and mesothelioma, an invariably fatal lung disease. Manville's managers suppressed the research. Moreover, as a matter of policy, they apparently decided to conceal the information from affected employees. The company's medical staff collaborated in the cover-up, for reasons we can only guess at.

Money may have been one motive. In one particularly chilling piece of testimony, a lawyer recalled how 40 years earlier he had confronted Manville's corporate counsel about the company's policy of concealing chest X-ray results from employees. The lawyer had asked, "Do you mean to tell me you would let them work until they dropped dead?" The reply was, "Yes, we save a lot of money that way."

Based on such testimony, a California court found that Manville had hidden the asbestos danger from its employees rather than looking for safer ways to handle it. It was less expensive to pay workers' compensation claims than to develop safer working conditions. A New Jersey court was even blunter: it found that Manville had made a conscious, cold-blooded business decision to take no protective or remedial action, in flagrant disregard of the rights of others.

How can we explain this behavior? Were more than 40 years' worth of Manville executives all immoral?

Such an answer defies common sense. The truth, I think, is less glamorous—and also less satisfying to those who like to explain evil as the actions of a few misbegotten souls. The people involved were probably ordinary men and women for the most part, not very different from you and me. They found themselves in a dilemma, and they solved it in a way that seemed to be the least troublesome, deciding not to disclose information that could hurt their product. The consequences of what they chose to do—both to thousands of innocent people and, ultimately, to the corporation—probably never occurred to them.

The Manville case illustrates the fine line between acceptable and unacceptable managerial behavior. Executives are expected to strike a difficult balance—to pursue their companies' best interests but not overstep the bounds of what outsiders will tolerate.

Even the best managers can find themselves in a bind, not knowing how far is too far. In retrospect, they can usually easily tell where they should have drawn the line, but no one manages in retrospect.We can only live and act today and hope that whoever looks back on what we did will judge that we struck the proper balance. In a few years, many of us may be found delinquent for decisions we are making now about tobacco, clean air, the use of chemicals, or some other seemingly benign substance.

The managers at Manville may have believed that they were acting in the company's best interests, or that what they were doing would never be found out, or even that it wasn't really wrong. In the end, these were only rationalizations for conduct that brought the company down.

CONTINENTAL ILLINOIS BANK

Until recently the ninth largest bank in the United States, Continental Illinois had to be saved from insolvency because of bad judgment by management. The government bailed it out, but at a price. In effect it has been socialized: about 80% of its equity now belongs to the Federal Deposit Insurance Corporation. Continental seems to have been brought down by managers who misunderstood its real interests. To their own peril, executives focused on a single-minded pursuit of corporate ends and forgot about the means to the ends.

In 1976, Continental's chairman declared that within five years the magnitude of its lending would match that of any other bank. The goal was attainable; in fact, for a time, Continental reached it. But it dictated a shift in strategy away from conservative corporate financing and toward aggressive pursuit of borrowers. So Continental, with lots of lendable funds, sent its loan officers into the field to buy loans that had originally been made by smaller banks that had less money.

The practice in itself was not necessarily unsound. But some of the smaller banks had done more than just lend money—they had swallowed hook, line, and sinker the extravagant, implausible dreams of poorly capitalized oil producers in Oklahoma, and they had begun to bet enormous sums on those dreams. Eventually, a cool billion dollars' worth of those dreams found their way into Continental's portfolio, and a cool billion dollars of depositors' money flowed out to pay for them. When the price of oil fell, a lot of dry holes and idle drilling equipment were all that was left to show for most of the money.

Continental's officers had become so entranced by their lending efforts' spectacular results that they hadn't looked deeply into how they had been achieved. Huge sums of money were lent at fat rates of interest. If the borrowers had been able to repay the loans, Continental might have become the eighth or even the seventh largest bank in the country. But that was a very big "if." Somehow there was a failure of control and judgment at Continental—probably because the officers who were buying those shaky loans were getting support and praise from their superiors. Or at least they were not hearing enough tough questions about them.

At one point, for example, Continental's internal auditors stumbled across the fact that an officer who had purchased $800 million in oil and gas loans from the Penn Square Bank in Oklahoma City had also borrowed $565,000 for himself from Penn Square. Continental's top management investigated and eventually issued a reprimand. The mild rebuke reflected the officer's hard work and the fact that the portfolio he had obtained would have yielded an average return of nearly 20% had it ever performed as planned. In fact, virtually all of the $800 million had to be written off. Management chose to interpret the incident charitably; federal prosecutors later alleged a kickback.

On at least two other occasions, Continental's own control mechanisms flashed signals that something was seriously wrong with the oil and gas portfolio. A vice president warned in a memo that the documentation needed to verify the soundness of many of the purchased loans had simply never arrived. Later, a junior loan officer, putting his job on the line, went over the heads of three superiors to tell a top executive about the missing documentation. Management chose not to investigate. After all, Continental was doing exactly what its chairman had said it would do: it was on its way to becoming the leading commercial lender in the United States. Oil and gas loans were an important factor in that achievement. Stopping to wait for paperwork to catch up would only slow down reaching the goal.

Eventually, however, the word got out about the instability of the bank's portfolio, which led to a massive run on its deposits. No other bank was willing to come to the rescue, for fear of being swamped by Continental's huge liabilities. To avoid going under, Continental in effect became a ward of the federal government. The losers were the bank's shareholders, some officers who lost their jobs, at least one who was indicted, and some 2,000 employees (about 15% of the total) who were let go, as the bank scaled down to fit its diminished assets.

Once again, it is easy for us to sit in judgment after the fact and say that Continental's loan officers and their superiors were doing exactly what bankers shouldn't do: they were gambling with their depositors' money. But on another level, this story is more difficult to analyze—and more generally a part of everyday business. Certainly part of Continental's problem was neglect of standard controls. But another dimension involved ambitious corporate goals. Pushed by lofty goals, managers could not see clearly their real interests. They focused on ends, overlooked the ethical questions associated with their choice of means—and ultimately hurt themselves.

E.F. HUTTON

The nation's second largest independent broker, E.F. Hutton & Company, recently pleaded guilty to 2,000 counts of mail and wire fraud. It had systematically bilked 400 of its banks by drawing against uncollected funds or in some cases against nonexistent sums, which it then covered after having enjoyed interest-free use of the money. So far, Hutton has agreed to pay a fine of $2 million as well as the government's investigation costs of $750,000. It has set up an $8 million reserve for restitution to the banks—which may not be enough. Several officers have lost their jobs, and some indictments may yet follow.

But worst of all, Hutton has tarnished its reputation, never a wise thing to do—certainly not when your business is offering to handle other people's money. Months after Hutton agreed to appoint new directors—as a way to give outsiders a solid majority on the board—the company couldn't find people to accept the seats, in part because of the bad publicity.

Apparently Hutton's branch managers had been encouraged to pay close attention to cash management. At some point, it dawned on someone that using other people's money was even more profitable than using your own. In each case, Hutton's overdrafts involved no large sums. But cumulatively, the savings on interest that would otherwise have been owed to the banks was very large. Because Hutton always made covering deposits, and because most banks did not object, Hutton assured its managers that what they were doing was sharp—and not shady. They presumably thought they were pushing legality to its limit without going over the line. The branch managers were simply taking full advantage of what the law and the bankers' tolerance permitted. On several occasions, the managers who played this game most astutely were even congratulated for their skill.

Hutton probably will not suffer a fate as drastic as Manville's or Continental Illinois's. Indeed, with astute damage control, it can probably emerge from this particular embarrassment with only a few bad memories. But this case has real value because it is typical of much corporate misconduct. Most improprieties don't cut a corporation off at the knees the way Manville's and Continental Illinois's did. In fact, most such actions are never revealed at all—or at least that's how people figure things will work out. And in many cases, a willingness to gamble thus is probably enhanced by the rationalization—true or not—that everyone else is doing something just as bad or would if they could; that those who wouldn't go for their share are idealistic fools.

Four Rationalizations

Why do managers do things that ultimately inflict great harm on their companies, themselves, and people on whose patronage or tolerance their organizations depend? These three cases, as well as the current crop of examples in each day's paper, supply ample evidence of the motivations and instincts that underlie corporate misconduct. Although the particulars may vary—from the gruesome dishonesty surrounding asbestos handling to the mundanity of illegal money management—the motivating beliefs are pretty much the same. We may examine them in the context of the corporation, but we know that these feelings are basic throughout society; we find them wherever we go because we take them with us.

When we look more closely at these cases, we can delineate four commonly held rationalizations that can lead to misconduct:

A belief that the activity is within reasonable ethical and legal limits—that is, that it is not "really" illegal or immoral.

A belief that the activity is in the individual's or the corporation's best interests—that the individual would somehow be expected to undertake the activity.

A belief that the activity is "safe" because it will never be found out or publicized; the classic crime-and-punishment issue of discovery.

A belief that because the activity helps the company the company will condone it and even protect the person who engages in it.

T HE IDEA THAT AN ACTION IS not really wrong is an old issue. How far is too far? Exactly where is the line between smart and too smart? Between sharp and shady? Between profit maximization and illegal conduct? The issue is complex: it involves an interplay between top management's goals and middle managers' efforts to interpret those aims.

Put enough people in an ambiguous, ill-defined situation, and some will conclude that whatever hasn't been labeled specifically wrong must be OK—especially if they are rewarded for certain acts. Deliberate overdrafts, for example, were not proscribed at Hutton. Since the company had not spelled out their illegality, it could later plead guilty for itself while shielding its employees from prosecution.

Top executives seldom ask their subordinates to do things that both of them know are against the law or imprudent. But company leaders sometimes leave things unsaid or give the impression that there are things they don't want to know about. In other words, they can seem, whether deliberately or otherwise, to be distancing themselves from their subordinates' tactical decisions in order to keep their own hands clean if things go awry. Often they lure ambitious lower level managers by implying that rich rewards await those who can produce certain results—and that the methods for achieving them will not be examined too closely. Continental's simple wrist-slapping of the officer who was caught in a flagrant conflict of interest sent a clear message to other managers about what top management really thought was important.

How can managers avoid crossing a line that is seldom precise? Unfortunately, most know that they have overstepped it only when they have gone too far. They have no reliable guidelines about what will be overlooked or tolerated or what will be condemned or attacked. When managers must operate in murky borderlands, their most reliable guideline is an old principle: when in doubt, don't.

That may seem like a timid way to run a business. One could argue that if it actually took hold among the middle managers who run most companies, it might take the enterprise out of free enterprise. But there is a difference between taking a worthwhile economic risk and risking an illegal act to make more money.

The difference between becoming a success and becoming a statistic lies in knowledge—including self-knowledge—not daring. Contrary to popular mythology, managers are not paid to take risks; they are paid to know which risks are worth taking. Also, maximizing profits is a company's second priority, not its first. The first is ensuring its survival.

All managers risk giving too much because of what their companies demand from them. But the same superiors who keep pressing you to do more, or to do it better, or faster, or less expensively, will turn on you should you cross that fuzzy line between right and wrong. They will blame you for exceeding instructions or for ignoring their warnings. The smartest managers already know that the best answer to the question, "How far is too far?" is don't try to find out.

T URNING TO THE SECOND REASON why people take risks that get their companies into trouble, believing that unethical conduct is in a person's or corporation's best interests nearly always results from a parochial view of what those interests are. For example, Alpha Industries, a Massachusetts manufacturer of microwave equipment, paid $57,000 to a Raytheon manager, ostensibly for a marketing report. Air force investigators charged that the report was a ruse to cover a bribe: Alpha wanted subcontracts that the Raytheon manager supervised. But those contracts ultimately cost Alpha a lot more than they paid for the report. After the company was indicted for bribery, its contracts were suspended and its profits promptly vanished. Alpha wasn't unique in this transgression: in 1984, the Pentagon suspended 453 other companies for violating procurement regulations.

Ambitious managers look for ways to attract favorable attention, something to distinguish them from other people. So they try to outperform their peers. Some may see that it is not difficult to look remarkably good in the short run by avoiding things that pay off only in the long run. For example, you can skimp on maintenance or training or customer service, and you can get away with it—for a while.

The sad truth is that many managers have been promoted on the basis of "great" results obtained in just those ways, leaving unfortunate successors to inherit the inevitable whirlwind. Since this is not necessarily a just world, the problems that such people create are not always traced back to them. Companies cannot afford to be hoodwinked in this way. They must be concerned with more than just results. They have to look very hard at how results are obtained.

Evidently, in Hutton's case there were such reviews, but management chose to interpret favorably what government investigators later interpreted unfavorably. This brings up another dilemma: management quite naturally hopes that any of its borderline actions will be overlooked or at least interpreted charitably if noticed. Companies must accept human nature for what it is and protect themselves with watchdogs to sniff out possible misdeeds.

An independent auditing agency that reports to outside directors can play such a role. It can provide a less comfortable, but more convincing, review of how management's successes are achieved. The discomfort can be considered inexpensive insurance and serve to remind all employees that the real interests of the company are served by honest conduct in the first place.

THE THIRD REASON WHY a risk is taken, believing that one can probably get away with it, is perhaps the most difficult to deal with because it's often true. A great deal of proscribed behavior escapes detection.

We know that conscience alone does not deter everyone. For example, First National Bank of Boston pleaded guilty to laundering satchels of $20 bills worth $1.3 billion. Thousands of satchels must have passed through the bank's doors without incident before the scheme was detected. That kind of heavy, unnoticed traffic breeds complacency.

How can we deter wrongdoing that is unlikely to be detected? Make it more likely to be detected. Had today's "discovery" process—in which plaintiff's attorneys can comb through a company's records to look for incriminating evidence—been in use when Manville concealed the evidence on asbestosis, there probably would have been no cover-up. Mindful of the likelihood of detection, Manville would have chosen a different course and could very well be thriving today without the protection of the bankruptcy courts.

The most effective deterrent is not to increase the severity of punishment for those caught but to heighten the perceived probability of being caught in the first place. For example, police have found that parking an empty patrol car at locations where motorists often exceed the speed limit reduces the frequency of speeding. Neighborhood "crime watch" signs that people display decrease burglaries.

Simply increasing the frequency of audits and spot checks is a deterrent, especially when combined with three other simple techniques: scheduling audits irregularly, making at least half of them unannounced, and setting up some checkups soon after others. But frequent spot checks cost more than big sticks, a fact that raises the question of which approach is more cost-effective.

A common managerial error is to assume that because frequent audits uncover little behavior that is out of line, less frequent, and therefore less costly, auditing is sufficient. But this condition overlooks the important deterrent effect of frequent checking. The point is to prevent misconduct, not just to catch it.

A trespass detected should not be dealt with discreetly. Managers should announce the misconduct and how the individuals involved were punished. Since the main deterrent to illegal or unethical behavior is the perceived probability of detection, managers should make an example of people who are detected.

Let's look at the fourth reason why corporate misconduct tends to occur, a belief that the company will condone actions that are taken in its interest and will even protect the managers responsible. The question we have to deal with here is, How do we keep company loyalty from going berserk?

That seems to be what happened at Manville. A small group of executives and a succession of corporate medical directors kept the facts about the lethal qualities of asbestos from becoming public knowledge for decades, and they managed to live with that knowledge. And at Manville, the company—or really, the company's senior management—did condone their decision and protect those employees.

Something similar seems to have happened at General Electric. When one of its missile projects ran up costs greater than the air force had agreed to pay, middle managers surreptitiously shifted those costs to projects that were still operating under budget. In this case, the loyalty that ran amok was primarily to the division: managers want their units' results to look good. But GE, with one of the finest reputations in U.S. industry, was splattered with scandal and paid a fine of $1.04 million.

One of the most troubling aspects of the GE case is the company's admission that those involved were thoroughly familiar with the company's ethical standards before the incident took place. This suggests that the practice of declaring codes of ethics and teaching them to managers is not enough to deter unethical conduct. Something stronger is needed.

Top management has a responsibility to exert a moral force within the company. Senior executives are responsible for drawing the line between loyalty to the company and action against the laws and values of the society in which the company must operate. Further, because that line can be obscured in the heat of the moment, the line has to be drawn well short of where reasonable men and women could begin to suspect that their rights had been violated. The company has to react long before a prosecutor, for instance, would have a strong enough case to seek an indictment.

Executives have a right to expect loyalty from employees against competitors and detractors, but not loyalty against the law, or against common morality, or against society itself. Managers must warn employees that a disservice to customers, and especially to innocent bystanders, cannot be a service to the company. Finally, and most important of all, managers must stress that excuses of company loyalty will not be accepted for acts that place its good name in jeopardy. To put it bluntly, superiors must make it clear that employees who harm other people allegedly for the company's benefit will be fired.

THE MOST EXTREME examples of corporate misconduct were due, in hindsight, to managerial failures. A good way to avoid management oversights is to subject the control mechanisms themselves to periodic surprise audits, perhaps as a function of the board of directors. The point is to make sure that internal audits and controls are functioning as planned. It's a case of inspecting the inspectors and taking the necessary steps to keep the controls working efficiently. Harold Geneen, former head of ITT, has suggested that the board should have an independent staff, something analogous to the Government Accounting Office, which reports to the legislative rather than the executive branch. In the end, it is up to top management to send a clear and pragmatic message to all employees that good ethics is still the foundation of good business.

Originally published in July–August 1986
Reprint 86402

Ethics in Practice

KENNETH R. ANDREWS

Executive Summary

WHY DO SO MANY APPARENTLY good people get snared in ethical problems at work—falsifying costs, for example, or concealing information about dangerous products? While some say it's the individual's fault, former HBR Editor Kenneth Andrews argues that ethical failures are management problems too. CEOs, directors, and other senior executives can readily raise their organizations' ethical standards—once they make up their minds to do so.

To Andrews, business ethics is a challenge with three parts: (1) developing managers as moral individuals; (2) building an environment in which standards and values are central to the company's strategy, just as economic purpose is; and (3) formulating and implementing policies that support ethical performance—as well as safeguards to assure that they are observed.

Rules and lectures alone, however, cannot create a moral company. The essence of management responsibility is the need to balance conflicting claims, to make decisions when there are no clear choices or absolute answers. In such situations, the character of the decision maker is decisive. And this is especially true when the decision maker is the CEO. That is why an explicit estimate of a candidate's character should be part of every management selection process.

Companies that are successful over time build their success on the creativity, the energy, and the will of their members. Such commitment cannot be sustained by strategic decisions that are ethically unsound.

As the 1990s overtake us, public interest in ethics is at a historic high. While the press calls attention to blatant derelictions on Wall Street, in the defense industry, and in the Pentagon, and to questionable activities in the White House, in the attorney general's office, and in Congress, observers wonder whether our society is sicker than usual. Probably not. The standards applied to corporate behavior have risen over time, and that has raised the average rectitude of businesspersons and politicians both. It has been a long time since we could say with Mark Twain that we have the best Senate money can buy or agree with muckrakers like Upton Sinclair that our large companies are the fiefdoms of robber barons. But illegal and unethical behavior persists, even as efforts to expose it often succeed in making its rewards short-lived.

Why do so many good people get caught falsifying costs?

Why is business ethics a problem that snares not just a few mature criminals or crooks in the making but a host of apparently good people who lead exemplary private lives while concealing information about dangerous products or systematically falsifying costs? My observation suggests that the problem of corporate ethics has three aspects: the development of the executive as a moral person; the influence of the corporation as a moral environment; and the actions needed to map a high road to economic and ethical performance—and to mount guardrails to keep corporate wayfarers on track.

Sometimes it is said that wrongdoing in business is an individual failure: a person of the proper moral fiber, properly brought up, simply would not cheat. Because of poor selection, a few bad apples are bound to appear in any big barrel. But these corporate misfits can subsequently be scooped out. Chief executive officers, we used to think, have a right to rely on the character of individual employees without being distracted from business objectives. Moral character is shaped by family, church, and education long before an individual joins a company to make a living.

In an ideal world, we might end here. In the real world, moral development is an unsolved problem at home, at school, at church—and at work. Two-career families, television, and the virtual disappearance of the dinner table as a forum for discussing moral issues have clearly outmoded instruction in basic principles at Mother's knee—if that fabled tutorial was ever as effective as folklore would have it. We cannot expect our battered school systems to take over the moral role of the family. Even religion is less help than it once might have

been when membership in a distinct community promoted—or coerced—conventional moral behavior. Society's increasing secularization, the profusion of sects, the
conservative church's divergence from new lifestyles,
pervasive distrust of the religious right—all these mean
that we cannot depend on uniform religious instruction
to armor business recruits against temptation.

Nor does higher education take up the slack, even in
disciplines in which moral indoctrination once flour-
ished. Great literature can be a self-evident source of ethical instruction, for it informs the mind and heart
together about the complexities of moral choice. Emo-
tionally engaged with fictional or historic characters who
must choose between death and dishonor, integrity and
personal advancement, power and responsibility, self
and others, we expand our own moral imaginations as
well. Yet professors of literature rarely offer guidance in
ethical interpretation, preferring instead to stress technical, aesthetic, or historical analysis.

Moral philosophy, which is the proper academic
home for ethical instruction, is even more remote, with
few professors choosing to teach applied ethics. When
you add to that the discipline's studied disengagement
from the world of practical affairs, it is not surprising
that most students (or managers) find little in the subject to attract them.

What does attract students—in large numbers—is
economics, with its theory of human behavior that
relates all motivation to personal pleasure, satisfaction,
and self-interest. And since self-interest is more easily
served than not by muscling aside the self-interest of
others, the Darwinian implications of conventional economic theory are essentially immoral. Competition produces and requires the will to win. Careerism focuses

attention on advantage. Immature individuals of all ages are prey to the moral flabbiness that William James said attends exclusive service to the bitch goddess Success.

Spurred in part by recent notorious examples of such flabbiness, many business schools are making determined efforts to reintroduce ethics in elective and required courses. But even if these efforts were further along than they are, boards of directors and senior managers would be unwise to assume that recruits could enter the corporate environment without need for additional education. The role of any school is to prepare its graduates for a lifetime of learning from experience that will go better and faster than it would have done without formal education. No matter how much colleges and business schools expand their investment in moral instruction, most education in business ethics (as in all other aspects of business acumen) will occur in the organizations in which people spend their lives.

M AKING ETHICAL DECISIONS is easy when the facts are clear and the choices black and white. But it is a different story when the situation is clouded by ambiguity, incomplete information, multiple points of view, and conflicting responsibilities. In such situations—which managers experience all the time—ethical decisions depend on both the decision-making process itself and on the experience, intelligence, and integrity of the decision maker.

Responsible moral judgment cannot be transferred to decision makers ready-made. Developing it in business turns out to be partly an administrative process involving: recognition of a decision's ethical implications; discussion to expose different points of view; and testing the tentative decision's adequacy in balancing self-interest and consideration of others, its import for future policy, and its consonance with the company's traditional values. But after all this, if a clear consensus has not emerged, then the executive in charge must decide, drawing on his or her intuition and conviction. This being so, the caliber of the decision maker is decisive—especially when an immediate decision must arise from instinct rather than from discussion.

This existential resolution requires the would-be moral individual to be the final authority in a situation where conflicting ethical principles are joined. It does not rule out prior consultation with others or recognition that, in a hierarchical organization, you might be overruled.

Ethical decisions therefore require of individuals three qualities that can be identified and developed. The first is competence to recognize ethical issues and to think through the consequences of alternative resolutions. The second is self-confidence to seek out different points of view and then to decide what is right at a given time and place, in a particular set of relationships and circumstances. The third is what William James called tough-mindedness, which in management is the willingness to make decisions when all that needs to be known cannot be known and when the questions that press for answers have no established and incontrovertible solutions.

Unfortunately, moral individuals in the modern corporation are too often on their own. But these individuals cannot be expected to remain autonomous, no matter how well endowed they are, without positive organized support. The stubborn persistence of ethical problems obscures the simplicity of the solution—once the leaders of a company decide to do something about their ethical standards. Ethical dereliction, sleaziness, or inertia is not merely an individual failure but a management problem as well.

When they first come to work, individuals whose moral judgment may ultimately determine their company's ethical character enter a community whose values will influence their own. The economic function of the corporation is necessarily one of those values. But if it is the only value, ethical inquiry cannot flourish. If management believes that the invisible hand of the market adequately moderates the injury done by the pursuit of self-interest, ethical policy can be dismissed as irrelevant. And if what people see (while they are hearing about maximizing shareholder wealth) are managers dedicated to their own survival and compensation, they will naturally be more concerned about rewards than about fairness.

For the individual, the impact of the need to succeed is doubtless more direct than the influence of neoclassical economic theory. But just as the corporation itself is saddled with the need to establish competitive advantage over time (after reinvestment of what could otherwise be the immediate profit by which the financial community and many shareholders judge its performance), aspiring managers will also be influenced by the way they are judged. A highly moral and humane chief executive can preside over an amoral organization because the incentive system focuses attention on short-term quantifiable results.

Under pressures to get ahead, the individual (of whose native integrity we are hopeful) is tempted to pursue advancement at the expense of others, to cut corners, to seek to win at all cost, to make things seem better than they are—to take advantage, in sum, of a myopic evaluation of performance. People will do what they are rewarded for doing. The quantifiable results of managerial activity are always much more visible than the quality and future consequences of the means by which they are attained.

By contrast, when the corporation is defined as a socioeconomic institution with responsibilities to other constituencies (employees, customers, and communities, for example), policy can be established to regulate the single-minded pursuit of maximum immediate profit. The leaders of such a company speak of social responsibility, promulgate ethical policy, and make their personal values available for emulation by their juniors. They are respectful of neoclassical economic theory, but find it only partially useful as a management guide.

As the corporation grows beyond its leader's daily direct influence, the ethical consequences of size and geographical deployment come into play. Control and enforcement of all policy becomes more difficult, but this is especially true with regard to policy established for corporate ethics. Layers of responsibility bring communication problems. The possibility of penalty engenders a lack of candor. Distance from headquarters complicates the evaluation of performance, driving it to numbers. When operations are dispersed among different cultures and countries in which corruption assumes exotic guises, a consensus about moral values is hard to achieve and maintain.

Moreover, decentralization in and of itself has ethical consequences, not least because it absolutely requires trust and latitude for error. The inability to monitor the performance of executives assigned to tasks their superiors cannot know in detail results inexorably in delegation.

Corporate leaders are accustomed to relying on the business acumen of profit-center managers, whose results the leaders watch with a practiced eye. Those concerned with maintaining their companies' ethical standards are just as dependent on the judgment and moral character of the managers to whom authority is delegated. Beyond keeping your fingers crossed, what can you do?

Fortunately for the future of the corporation, this microcosm of society can be, within limits, what its leadership and membership make it. The corporation is an organization in which people influence one another to establish accepted values and ways of doing things. It is not a democracy, but to be fully effective, the authority of its leaders must be supported by their followers. Its leadership has more power than elected officials do to choose who will join or remain in the association. Its members expect direction to be proposed even as they threaten resistance to change. Careless or lazy managements let their organizations drift, continuing their economic performance along lines previously established and leaving their ethics to chance. Resolute managements find they can surmount the problems I have dwelt on—once they have separated these problems from their camouflage.

It is possible to carve out of our pluralistic, multicultured society a coherent community with a strategy that defines both its economic purposes and the standards of competence, quality, and humanity that govern its activities. The character of a corporation may well be more malleable than an individual's. Certainly its culture can be shaped. Intractable persons can be replaced or retired. Those committed to the company's goals can generate formal and informal sanctions to constrain and alienate those who are not.

Shaping such a community begins with the personal influence of the chief executive and that of the managers who are heads of business *How can you tell* units, staff departments, or *whether managers merit* any other suborganizations *your trust?* to which authority is delegated. The determination of explicit ethical policy comes next, followed by the same management procedures that are used to execute any body of policy in effective organizations.

The way the chief executive exercises moral judgment is universally acknowledged to be more influential than written policy. The CEO who orders the immediate recall of a product, at the cost of millions of dollars in sales because of a quality defect affecting a limited number of untraceable shipments, sends one kind of message. The executive who suppresses information about a producer's actual or potential ill effects or, knowingly or not, condones overcharging, sends another.

Policy is implicit in behavior. The ethical aspects of product quality, personnel, advertising, and marketing decisions are immediately plain. CEOs say much more than they know in the most casual contacts with those who watch their every move. Pretense is futile. "Do not *say* things," Emerson once wrote. "What you *are* stands over you the while, and thunders so that I can not hear what you say to the contrary." It follows that "if you would not be known to do anything, never do it."

The modest person might respond to this attribution of transparency with a "who, me?" Self-confident sophisticates will refuse to consider themselves so easily read.

Almost all executives underestimate their power and do not recognize deference in others. The import of this, of course, is that a CEO should be conscious of how the position amplifies his or her most casual judgments, jokes, and silences. But an even more important implication—given that people cannot hide their characters—is that the selection of a chief executive (indeed of any aspirant to management responsibility) should include an explicit estimate of his or her character. If you ask how to do that, Emerson would reply, "Just look."

O NCE A COMPANY'S LEADERS have decided that its ethical intentions and performance will be managed, rather than left untended in the corrosive environment of unprincipled competition, they must determine their corporate policy and make it explicit much as they do in other areas. The need for written policy is especially urgent in companies without a strong tradition to draw on or where a new era must be launched—after a public scandal, say, or an internal investigation of questionable behavior. Codes of ethics are now commonplace. But in and of themselves they are not effective, and this is especially true when they are so broadly stated that they can be dismissed as merely cosmetic.

Internal policies specifically addressed to points of industry, company, and functional vulnerability make compliance easier to audit and training easier to conduct. Where particular practices are of major concern— price fixing, for example, or bribery of government officials or procurement—compliance can be made a condition of employment and certified annually by employees' signatures. Still, the most pervasive problems cannot be foreseen, nor can the proper procedures be so spelled out in advance as to tell the person on the line what to do. Unreasonably repressive rules undermine trust, which remains indispensable.

What executives can do is advance awareness of the kinds of problems that are foreseeable. Since policy cannot be effective unless it is understood, some companies use corporate training sessions to discuss the problems of applying their ethical standards. In difficult situations, judgment in making the leap from general policy statements to situationally specific action can be informed by discussion. Such discussion, if carefully conducted, can reveal the inadequacy or ambiguity of present policy, new areas in which the company must take a unified stand, and new ways to support individuals in making the right decisions.

As in all policy formulation and implementation, the deportment of the CEO, the development of relevant policy—and training in its meaning and application —are not enough. In companies determined to sustain or raise ethical standards, management expands the information system to illuminate pressure points—the rate of manufacturing defects, product returns and warranty claims, special instances of quality shortfalls, results of competitive benchmarking inquiries—whatever makes good sense in the special circumstances of the company.

Because trust is indispensable, ethical aspirations must be supported by information that serves not only to inform but also to control. Control need not be so much coercive as customary, representing not suspicion but a normal interest in the quality of operations. Experienced executives do not substitute trust for the awareness that policy is often distorted in practice. Ample information, like full visibility, is a powerful deterrent.

This is why purposely ethical organizations expand the traditional sphere of external and internal audits (which is wherever fraud may occur) to include compliance with corporate ethical standards. Even more important, such organizations pay attention to every kind of obstacle that limits performance and to problems needing ventilation so that help can be provided.

To obtain information that is deeply guarded to avoid penalty, internal auditors—long since taught not to prowl about as police or detectives—must be people with enough management experience to be sensitive to the manager's need for economically viable decisions. For example, they should have imagination enough to envision ethical outcomes from bread-and-butter profit and pricing decisions, equal opportunity and payoff dilemmas, or downsizing crunches. Establishing an audit and control climate that takes as a given an open exchange of information between the company's operating levels and policy-setting levels is not difficult—once, that is, the need to do so is recognized and persons of adequate experience and respect are assigned to the work.

But no matter how much empathy audit teams exhibit, discipline ultimately requires action. The secretary who steals petty cash, the successful salesman who falsifies his expense account, the accountant and her boss who alter cost records, and, more problematically, the chronically sleazy operator who never does anything actually illegal—all must be dealt with cleanly, with minimum attention to allegedly extenuating circumstances. It is true that hasty punishment may be unjust and absolve superiors improperly of their secondary responsibility for wrongdoing. But long delay or waffling in the effort to be humane obscures the message the organization requires whenever violations occur. Trying to conceal a major lapse or safeguarding the names of people who have been fired is kind to the offender but blunts the salutary impact of disclosure.

For the executive, the administration of discipline incurs one ethical dilemma after another: How do you weigh consideration for the offending individual, for example, and how do you weigh the future of the organization? A company dramatizes its uncompromising adherence to lawful and ethical behavior when it severs employees who commit offenses that were classified in advance as unforgivable. When such a decision is fair, the grapevine makes its equity clear even when more formal publicity is inappropriate. Tough decisions should not be postponed simply because they are painful. The steady support of corporate integrity is never without emotional cost.

In a large, decentralized organization, consistently ethical performance requires difficult decisions from not only the current CEO but also a succession of chief executives. Here the board of directors enters the scene. The board has the opportunity to provide for a succession of CEOs whose personal values and characters are consistently adequate for sustaining and developing established traditions for ethical conduct. Once in place, chief executives must rely on two resources for getting done what they cannot do personally: the character of their associates and the influence of policy and the measures that are taken to make policy effective.

An adequate corporate strategy must include noneconomic goals. An economic strategy is the optimal match of a company's product and market opportunities with its resources and distinctive competence. (That both are continually changing is of course true.) But economic strategy is humanized and made attainable by deciding what kind of organization the company will be—its character, the values it espouses, its relationships to customers, employees, communities, and shareholders. The personal values and ethical aspirations of the company's leaders, though probably not specifically stated, are implicit in all strategic decisions. They show through the choices management makes and reveal themselves as the company goes about its business. That is why this communication should be deliberate and purposeful rather than random.

Although codes of ethics, ethical policy for specific vulnerabilities, and disciplined enforcement are important, they do not contain in themselves the final emotional power of commitment. Commitment to quality objectives—among them compliance with law and high ethical standards—is an organizational achievement. It is inspired by pride more than by the profit that rightful pride produces. Once the scope of strategic decisions is thus enlarged, their ethical component is no longer at odds with a decision right for many reasons.

As FORMER EDITOR OF HBR, I am acutely aware of how difficult it is to persuade businesspeople to write or speak about corporate ethics. I am not comfortable doing so myself. To generalize the ethical aspects of a business decision, leaving behind the concrete particulars that make it real, is too often to sermonize, to simplify, or to rationalize away the plain fact that many instances of competing ethical claims have no satisfactory solution. But we also hear little public comment from business leaders of integrity when incontestable breaches of conduct are made known—and silence suggests to cynics an absence of concern.

The impediments to explicit discussion of ethics in business are many, beginning with the chief executive's keen awareness that someday he or she may be betrayed by someone in his or her own organization. Moral exhortation and oral piety are offensive, especially when attended by hypocrisy or real vulnerability to criticism. Any successful or energetic individual will sometime encounter questions about his or her methods and motives, for even well-intentioned behavior may be judged unethical from some point of view. The need for cooperation among people with different beliefs diminishes discussion of religion and related ethical issues. That persons with management responsibility must find the principles to resolve conflicting ethical claims in their own minds and hearts is an unwelcome discovery. Most of us keep quiet about it.

Ultimately, executives resolve conflicting claims in their own minds and hearts.

In summary, my ideas are quite simple. Perhaps the most important is that management's total loyalty to the maximization of profit is the principal obstacle to achieving higher standards of ethical practice. Defining the purpose of the corporation as exclusively economic is a deadly oversimplification, which allows overemphasis on self-interest at the expense of consideration of others.

The practice of management requires a prolonged play of judgment. Executives must find in their own will, experience, and intelligence the principles they apply in balancing conflicting claims. Wise men and women will submit their views to others, for open discussion of problems reveals unsuspected ethical dimensions and develops alternative viewpoints that should be taken into account. Ultimately, however, executives must make a decision, relying on their own judgment to settle infinitely debatable issues. Inquiry into character should therefore be part of all executive selection—as well as all executive development within the corporation.

And so it goes. That much and that little. The encouraging outcome is that promulgating and institutionalizing ethical policy are not so difficult as, for example, escaping the compulsion of greed. Once undertaken, the process can be as straightforward as the articulation and implementation of policy in any sphere. Any company has the opportunity to develop a unique corporate strategy summarizing its chief purposes and policies. That strategy can encompass not only the economic role it will play in national and international markets but also the kind of company it will be as a human organization. It will embrace as well, though perhaps not publicly, the nature and scope of the leadership to which the company is to be entrusted.

To be implemented successfully over time, any strategy must command the creativity, energy, and desire of the company's members. Strategic decisions that are economically or ethically unsound will not long sustain such commitment.

Originally published in September–October 1989
Reprint 89501

Managing for Organizational Integrity

LYNN SHARP PAINE

Executive Summary

ETHICS, ARGUES LYNN SHARP PAINE, is as much an organizational as a personal issue. And managers who fail to provide leadership and institute systems that facilitate ethical conduct share responsibility with those who knowingly benefit from corporate misdeeds.

Executives who ignore ethics run the risk of personal and corporate liability in an increasingly tough legal environment. In addition, they deprive their organizations of the benefits available under new federal guidelines that recognize for the first time the organizational and managerial roots of unlawful conduct and base fines partly on the extent to which companies have taken steps to prevent that misconduct. Prompted by the prospect of leniency, many companies are rushing to implement compliance-based ethics programs. Designed by corporate counsel, the goal of these programs is to prevent, detect, and punish legal violations. But to foster a climate that encourages exemplary behavior, corporations need more.

An integrity-based approach to ethics management combines a concern for the law with an emphasis on managerial responsibility for ethical behavior. While integrity strategies may vary in design and scope, all strive to define companies' guiding values, aspirations, and patterns of thoughts and conduct. When integrated into the day-to-day operations of a company, such strategies can help prevent damaging ethical lapses, while tapping into powerful human impulses for moral thought and action.

Many managers think of ethics as a question of personal scruples, a confidential matter between individuals and their consciences. These executives are quick to describe any wrongdoing as an isolated incident, the work of a rogue employee. The thought that the company could bear any responsibility for an individual's misdeeds never enters their minds. Ethics, after all, has nothing to do with management.

In fact, ethics has *everything* to do with management. Rarely do the character flaws of a lone actor fully explain corporate misconduct. More typically, unethical business practice involves the tacit, if not explicit, cooperation of others and reflects the values, attitudes, beliefs, language, and behavioral patterns that define an organization's operating culture. Ethics, then, is as much an organizational as a personal issue. Managers who fail to provide proper leadership and to institute systems that facilitate ethical conduct share responsibility with those who conceive, execute, and knowingly benefit from corporate misdeeds.

Managers must acknowledge their role in shaping organizational ethics and seize this opportunity to create a climate that can strengthen the relationships and reputations on which their companies' success depends. Executives who ignore ethics run the risk of personal and corporate liability in today's increasingly tough legal environment. In addition, they deprive their organizations of the benefits available under new federal guidelines for sentencing organizations convicted of wrongdoing. These sentencing guidelines recognize for the first time the organizational and managerial roots of unlawful conduct and base fines partly on the extent to which companies have taken steps to prevent that misconduct.

Prompted by the prospect of leniency, many companies are rushing to implement compliance-based ethics programs. Designed by corporate counsel, the goal of these programs is to prevent, detect, and punish legal violations. But organizational ethics means more than avoiding illegal practice; and providing employees with a rule book will do little to address the problems underlying unlawful conduct. To foster a climate that encourages exemplary behavior, corporations need a comprehensive approach that goes beyond the often punitive legal compliance stance.

An integrity-based approach to ethics management combines a concern for the law with an emphasis on managerial responsibility for ethical behavior. Though integrity strategies may vary in design and scope, all strive to define companies' guiding values, aspirations, and patterns of thought and conduct. When integrated into the day-to-day operations of an organization, such strategies can help prevent damaging ethical lapses while tapping into powerful human impulses for moral thought and action. Then an ethical framework becomes no longer a burdensome constraint within which companies must operate, but the governing ethos of an organization.

How Organizations Shape Individuals' Behavior

The once familiar picture of ethics as individualistic, unchanging, and impervious to organizational influences has not stood up to scrutiny in recent years. Sears Auto Centers' and Beech-Nut Nutrition Corporation's experiences illustrate the role organizations play in shaping individuals' behavior—and how even sound moral fiber can fray when stretched too thin.

In 1992, Sears, Roebuck & Company was inundated with complaints about its automotive service business. Consumers and attorneys general in more than 40 states had accused the company of misleading customers and selling them unnecessary parts and services, from brake jobs to front-end alignments. It would be a mistake, however, to see this situation exclusively in terms of any one individual's moral failings. Nor did management set out to defraud Sears customers. Instead, a number of organizational factors contributed to the problematic sales practices.

In the face of declining revenues, shrinking market share, and an increasingly competitive market for under-car services, Sears management attempted to spur the performance of its auto centers by introducing new goals and incentives for employees. The company increased minimum work quotas and introduced productivity incentives for mechanics. The automotive service advisers were given product-specific sales quotas—sell so many springs, shock absorbers, alignments, or brake jobs per shift—and paid a commission based on sales. According to advisers, failure to meet quotas could lead to a transfer or a reduction in work hours. Some employees spoke of the "pressure, pressure, pressure" to bring in sales.

Under this new set of organizational pressures and incentives, with few options for meeting their sales goals legitimately, some employees' judgment understandably suffered. Management's failure to clarify the line between unnecessary service and legitimate preventive maintenance, coupled with consumer ignorance, left employees to chart their own courses through their own courses through a vast gray area, subject to a wide range of interpretations. Without active management support for ethical practice and mechanisms to detect and check questionable sales methods and poor work, it is not surprising that some employees may have reacted to contextual forces by resorting to exaggeration, carelessness, or even misrepresentation.

At Sears Auto Centers, management's failure to clarify the line between unnecessary service and legitimate preventive maintenance cost the company an estimated $60 million.

Shortly after the allegations against Sears became public, CEO Edward Brennan acknowledged management's responsibility for putting in place compensation and goal-setting systems that "created an environment in which mistakes did occur." Although the company denied any intent to deceive consumers, senior executives eliminated commissions for service advisers and discontinued sales quotas for specific parts. They also instituted a system of unannounced shopping audits and made plans to expand the internal monitoring of service. In settling the pending lawsuits, Sears offered coupons to customers who had bought certain auto services between 1990 and 1992. The total cost of the settlement, including potential customer refunds, was an estimated $60 million.

Contextual forces can also influence the behavior of top management, as a former CEO of Beech-Nut Nutrition Corporation discovered. In the early 1980s, only two years after joining the company, the CEO found evidence suggesting that the apple juice concentrate, supplied by the company's vendors for use in Beech-Nut's "100% pure" apple juice, contained nothing more than sugar water and chemicals. The CEO could have destroyed the bogus inventory and withdrawn the juice from grocers' shelves, but he was under extraordinary pressure to turn the ailing company around. Eliminating the inventory would have killed any hope of turning even the meager $700,000 profit promised to Beech-Nut's then-parent, Nestlé.

When a Beech-Nut employee voiced concerns about the purity of apple juice concentrate, he was accused of not being a team player.

A number of people in the corporation, it turned out, had doubted the purity of the juice for several years before the CEO arrived. But the 25% price advantage offered by the supplier of the bogus concentrate allowed the operations head to meet cost-control goals. Furthermore, the company lacked an effective quality control system, and a conclusive lab test for juice purity did not yet exist. When a member of the research department voiced concerns about the juice to operating management, he was accused of not being a team player and of acting like "Chicken Little." His judgment, his supervisor wrote in an annual performance review, was "colored by naïveté and impractical ideals." No one else seemed to

have considered the company's obligations to its customers or to have thought about the potential harm of
disclosure. No one considered the fact that the sale of
adulterated or misbranded juice is a legal offense,
putting the company and its top management at risk of
criminal liability.

An FDA investigation taught Beech-Nut the hard way.
In 1987, the company pleaded guilty to selling adulterated and misbranded juice. Two years and two criminal
trials later, the CEO pleaded guilty to ten counts of mis-
labeling. The total cost to the company—including fines,
legal expenses, and lost sales—was an estimated
$25 million.

Such errors of judgment rarely reflect an organizational culture and management philosophy that sets out
to harm or deceive. More often, they reveal a culture that
is insensitive or indifferent to ethical considerations or
one that lacks effective organizational systems. By the
same token, exemplary conduct usually reflects an organizational culture and philosophy that is infused with a
sense of responsibility.

For example, Johnson & Johnson's handling of the
Tylenol crisis is sometimes attributed to the singular
personality of then-CEO
James Burke. However, the
decision to do a nationwide
recall of Tylenol capsules in
order to avoid further loss of
life from product tampering
was in reality not one decision but thousands of deci-
sions made by individuals at all levels of the organization. The "Tylenol decision," then, is best understood not
as an isolated incident, the achievement of a lone individual, but as the reflection of an organization's culture.

Acknowledging the importance of organizational context in ethics does not imply forgiving individual wrongdoers.

Without a shared set of values and guiding principles deeply ingrained throughout the organization, it is doubtful that Johnson & Johnson's response would have been as rapid, cohesive, and ethically sound.

Many people resist acknowledging the influence of organizational factors on individual behavior—especially on misconduct—for fear of diluting people's sense of personal moral responsibility. But this fear is based on a false dichotomy between holding individual transgressors accountable and holding "the system" accountable. Acknowledging the importance of organizational context need not imply exculpating individual wrongdoers. To understand all is not to forgive all.

The Limits of a Legal Compliance Program

The consequences of an ethical lapse can be serious and far-reaching. Organizations can quickly become entangled in an all-consuming web of legal proceedings. The risk of litigation and liability has increased in the past decade as lawmakers have legislated new civil and criminal offenses, stepped up penalties, and improved support for law enforcement. Equally—if not more—important is the damage an ethical lapse can do to an organization's reputation and relationships. Both Sears and Beech-Nut, for instance, struggled to regain consumer trust and market share long after legal proceedings had ended.

As more managers have become alerted to the importance of organizational ethics, many have asked their lawyers to develop corporate ethics programs to detect and prevent violations of the law. The 1991 Federal Sentencing Guidelines offer a compelling rationale. Sanctions such as fines and probation for organizations convicted of wrongdoing can vary dramatically depending both on the degree of management cooperation in reporting and investigating corporate misdeeds and on whether or not the company has implemented a legal compliance program. (See "Corporate Fines Under the Federal Sentencing Guidelines" at the end of this article.)

Such programs tend to emphasize the prevention of unlawful conduct, primarily by increasing surveillance and control and by imposing penalties for wrongdoers. While plans vary, the basic framework is outlined in the sentencing guidelines. Managers must establish compliance standards and procedures; designate high-level personnel to oversee compliance; avoid delegating discretionary authority to those likely to act unlawfully; effectively communicate the company's standards and procedures through training or publications; take reasonable steps to achieve compliance through audits, monitoring processes, and a system for employees to report criminal misconduct without fear of retribution; consistently enforce standards through appropriate disciplinary measures; respond appropriately when offenses are detected; and, finally, take reasonable steps to prevent the occurrence of similar offenses in the future.

There is no question of the necessity of a sound, well-articulated strategy for legal compliance in an organization. After all, employees can be frustrated and frightened by the complexity of today's legal environment. And even managers who claim to use the law as a guide to ethical behavior often lack more than a rudimentary understanding of complex legal issues.

Managers would be mistaken, however, to regard legal compliance as an adequate means for addressing the full range of ethical issues that arise every day. "If it's legal, it's ethical," is a frequently heard slogan. But conduct that is lawful may be highly problematic from an ethical point of view. Consider the sale in some countries of hazardous products without appropriate warnings or the purchase of goods from suppliers who operate inhumane sweatshops in developing countries. Companies engaged in international business often discover that conduct that infringes on recognized standards of human rights and decency is legally permissible in some jurisdictions.

Legal clearance does not certify the absence of ethical problems in the United States either, as a 1991 case at Salomon Brothers illustrates. Four top-level executives failed to take appropriate action when learning of unlawful activities on the government trading desk. Company lawyers found no law obligating the executives to disclose the improprieties. Nevertheless, the executives' delay in disclosing and failure to reveal their prior knowledge prompted a serious crisis of confidence among employees, creditors, shareholders, and customers. The executives were forced to resign, having lost the moral authority to lead. Their ethical lapse compounded the trading desk's legal offenses, and the company ended up suffering losses—including legal costs, increased funding costs, and lost business—estimated at nearly $1 billion.

A compliance approach to ethics also overemphasizes the threat of detection and punishment in order to channel behavior in lawful directions. The underlying model for this approach is deterrence theory, which envisions people as rational maximizers of self-interest, responsive to the personal costs and benefits of their choices, yet indifferent to the moral legitimacy of those choices. But a recent study reported in *Why People Obey the Law* by Tom R. Tyler shows that obedience to the law is strongly influenced by a belief in its legitimacy and its moral correctness. People generally feel that they have a strong obligation to obey the law. Education about the legal standards and a supportive environment may be all that's required to insure compliance.

Discipline is, of course, a necessary part of any ethical system. Justified penalties for the infringement of legitimate norms are fair and appropriate. Some people do need the threat of sanctions. However, an overemphasis on potential sanctions can be superfluous and even counterproductive. Employees may rebel against programs that stress penalties, particularly if they are designed and imposed without employee involvement

Management may talk of mutual trust when unveiling a compliance plan, but employees often see a warning from on high.

or if the standards are vague or unrealistic. Management may talk of mutual trust when unveiling a compliance plan, but employees often receive the message as a warning from on high. Indeed, the more skeptical among them may view compliance programs as nothing more than liability insurance for senior management. This is not an unreasonable conclusion, considering that compliance programs rarely address the root causes of misconduct.

Even in the best cases, legal compliance is unlikely to unleash much moral imagination or commitment. The law does not generally seek to inspire human excellence or distinction. It is no guide for exemplary behavior—or even good practice. Those managers who define ethics as legal compliance are implicitly endorsing a code of moral mediocrity for their organizations. As Richard Breeden, former chairman of the Securities and Exchange Commission, noted, "It is not an adequate ethical standard to aspire to get through the day without being indicted."

Integrity as a Governing Ethic

A strategy based on integrity holds organizations to a more robust standard. While compliance is rooted in avoiding legal sanctions, organizational integrity is based on the concept of self-governance in accordance with a set of guiding principles. From the perspective of integrity, the task of ethics management is to define and give life to an organization's guiding values, to create an environment that supports ethically sound behavior, and to instill a sense of shared accountability among employees. The need to obey the law is viewed as a positive aspect of organizational life, rather than an unwelcome constraint imposed by external authorities.

An integrity strategy is characterized by a conception of ethics as a driving force of an enterprise. Ethical values shape the search for opportunities, the design of organizational systems, and the decision-making process used by individuals and groups. They provide a common frame of reference and serve as a unifying force across different functions, lines of business, and employee groups. Organizational ethics helps define what a company is and what it stands for.

Many integrity initiatives have structural features common to compliance-based initiatives: a code of conduct, training in relevant areas of law, mechanisms for reporting and investigating potential misconduct, and audits and controls to insure that laws and company standards are being met. In addition, if suitably designed, an integrity-based initiative can establish a foundation for seeking the legal benefits that are available under the sentencing guidelines should criminal wrongdoing occur. (See "The Hallmarks of an Effective Integrity Strategy" at the end of this article.)

But an integrity strategy is broader, deeper, and more demanding than a legal compliance initiative. Broader in that it seeks to enable responsible conduct. Deeper in that it cuts to the ethos and operating systems of the organization and its members, their guiding values and patterns of thought and action. And more demanding in that it requires an active effort to define the responsibilities and aspirations that constitute an organization's ethical compass. Above all, organizational ethics is seen as the work of management. Corporate counsel may play a role in the design and implementation of integrity strategies, but managers at all levels and across all functions are involved in the process. (See the chart, "Strategies for Ethics Management.")

During the past decade, a number of companies have undertaken integrity initiatives. They vary according to the ethical values focused on and the implementation approaches used. Some companies focus on the core values of integrity that reflect basic social obligations, such as respect for the rights of others, honesty, fair dealing, and obedience to the law. Other companies emphasize aspirations—values that are ethically desirable but not necessarily morally obligatory—such as good service to customers, a commitment to diversity, and involvement in the community.

When it comes to implementation, some companies begin with behavior. Following Aristotle's view that one becomes courageous by acting as a courageous person, such companies develop codes of conduct specifying appropriate behavior, along with a system of incentives, audits, and controls. Other companies focus less on specific actions and more on developing attitudes, decision-making processes, and ways of thinking that reflect their values. The assumption is that personal commitment and appropriate decision processes will lead to right action.

Martin Marietta, NovaCare, and Wetherill Associates have implemented and lived with quite different integrity strategies. In each case, management has found that the initiative has made important and often unexpected contributions to competitiveness, work environ-

---

Strategies for Ethics Management

Characteristics of Compliance Strategy

Ethos	conformity with externally imposed standards
Objective	prevent criminal misconduct
Leadership	lawyer driven
Methods	education, reduced discretion, auditing and controls, penalties
Behavioral Assumptions	autonomous beings guided by material self-interest

Implementation of Compliance Strategy

Standards	criminal and regulatory law
Staffing	lawyers
Activities	develop compliance standards train and communicate handle reports of misconduct conduct investigations oversee compliance audits enforce standards
Education	compliance standards and system

ment, and key relationships on which the company depends.

Martin Marietta: Emphasizing Core Values

Martin Marietta Corporation, the U.S. aerospace and defense contractor, opted for an integrity-based ethics

---

Characteristics of Integrity Strategy

Ethos	self-governance according to chosen standards
Objective	enable responsible conduct
Leadership	management driven with aid of lawyers, HR, others
Methods	education, leadership, accountability, organizational systems and decision processes, auditing and controls, penalties
Behavioral Assumptions	social beings guided by material self-interest, values, ideals, peers

Implementation of Integrity Strategy

Standards	company values and aspirations social obligations, including law
Staffing	executives and managers with lawyers, others
Activities	lead development of company values and standards train and communicate integrate into company systems provide guidance and consultation assess values performance identify and resolve problems oversee compliance activities
Education	decision making and values compliance standards and system

program in 1985. At the time, the defense industry was
under attack for fraud and mismanagement, and Martin
Marietta was under investigation for improper travel
billings. Managers knew they needed a better form of
self-governance but were skeptical that an ethics program could influence behavior. "Back then people asked,
'Do you really need an ethics program to be ethical?'"
recalls current President Thomas Young. "Ethics was
something personal. Either you had it, or you didn't."

The corporate general counsel played a pivotal role in
promoting the program, and legal compliance was a critical objective. But it was conceived of and implemented
from the start as a companywide management initiative
aimed at creating and maintaining a "do-it-right" climate. In its original conception, the program empha-
sized core values, such as honesty and fair play. Over
time, it expanded to encompass quality and environmental responsibility as well.

Today the initiative consists of a code of conduct, an
ethics training program, and procedures for reporting
and investigating ethical concerns within the company.
It also includes a system for disclosing violations of federal procurement law to the government. A corporate
ethics office manages the program, and ethics representatives are stationed at major facilities. An ethics steering committee, made up of Martin Marietta's president,
senior executives, and two rotating members selected
from field operations, oversees the ethics office. The
audit and ethics committee of the board of directors
oversees the steering committee.

The ethics office is responsible for responding to
questions and concerns from the company's employees.
Its network of representatives serves as a sounding
board, a source of guidance, and a channel for raising a
range of issues, from allegations of wrongdoing to com-

plaints about poor management, unfair supervision, and company policies and practices. Martin Marietta's ethics

Martin Marietta's ethics training program teaches senior executives how to balance responsibilities.

network, which accepts anonymous complaints, logged over 9,000 calls in 1991, when the company had about 60,000 employees. In 1992, it investigated 684 cases. The ethics office also works closely with the human resources, legal, audit, communications, and security functions to respond to employee concerns.

Shortly after establishing the program, the company began its first round of ethics training for the entire workforce, starting with the CEO and senior executives. Now in its third round, training for senior executives focuses on decision making, the challenges of balancing multiple responsibilities, and compliance with laws and regulations critical to the company. The incentive compensation plan for executives makes responsibility for promoting ethical conduct an explicit requirement for reward eligibility and requires that business and personal goals be achieved in accordance with the company's policy on ethics. Ethical conduct and support for the ethics program are also criteria in regular performance reviews.

Today top-level managers say the ethics program has helped the company avoid serious problems and become more responsive to its more than 90,000 employees. The ethics network, which tracks the number and types of cases and complaints, has served as an early warning system for poor management, quality and safety defects, racial and gender discrimination, environmental concerns, inaccurate and false records, and personnel grievances regarding salaries, promotions, and layoffs. By providing an alternative channel for raising such concerns, Martin Marietta is able to take corrective action more quickly and with a lot less pain. In many cases, potentially embarrassing problems have been identified and dealt with before becoming a management crisis, a lawsuit, or a criminal investigation. Among employees who brought complaints in 1993, 75% were satisfied with the results.

Company executives are also convinced that the program has helped reduce the incidence of misconduct. When allegations of misconduct do surface, the company says it deals with them more openly. On several occasions, for instance, Martin Marietta has voluntarily disclosed and made restitution to the government for misconduct involving potential violations of federal procurement laws. In addition, when an employee alleged that the company had retaliated against him for voicing safety concerns about his plant on CBS news, top management commissioned an investigation by an outside law firm. Although failing to support the allegations, the investigation found that employees at the plant feared retaliation when raising health, safety, or environmental complaints. The company redoubled its efforts to identify and discipline those employees taking retaliatory action and stressed the desirability of an open work environment in its ethics training and company communications.

Although the ethics program helps Martin Marietta avoid certain types of litigation, it has occasionally led to other kinds of legal action. In a few cases, employees dismissed for violating the code of ethics sued Martin Marietta, arguing that the company had violated its own code by imposing unfair and excessive discipline.

Still, the company believes that its attention to ethics has been worth it. The ethics program has led to better relationships with the government, as well as to new business opportunities. Along with prices and technology, Martin Marietta's record of integrity, quality, and reliability of estimates plays a role in the awarding of defense contracts, which account for some 75% of the company's revenues. Executives believe that the reputation they've earned through their ethics program has helped them build trust with government auditors, as well. By opening up communications, the company has reduced the time spent on redundant audits.

The program has also helped change employees' perceptions and priorities. Some managers compare their new ways of thinking about ethics to the way they understand quality. They consider more carefully how situations will be perceived by others, the possible long-term consequences of short-term thinking, and the need for continuous improvement. CEO Norman Augustine notes, "Ten years ago, people would have said that there were no ethical issues in business. Today employees think their number-one objective is to be thought of as decent people doing quality work."

NovaCare: Building Shared Aspirations

NovaCare Inc., one of the largest providers of rehabilitation services to nursing homes and hospitals in the United States, has oriented its ethics effort toward building a common core of shared aspirations. But in 1988, when the company was called InSpeech, the only sentiment shared was mutual mistrust.

Senior executives built the company from a series of aggressive acquisitions over a brief period of time to take advantage of the expanding market for therapeutic services. However, in 1988, the viability of the company was

in question. Turnover among its frontline employees—
the clinicians and therapists who care for patients in
nursing homes and hospitals—escalated to 57% per year.
The company's inability to retain therapists caused customers to defect and the stock price to languish in an
extended slump.

After months of soul-searching, InSpeech executives
realized that the turnover rate was a symptom of a more
basic problem: the lack of a common set of values and
aspirations. There was, as one executive put it, a "huge
disconnect" between the values
of the therapists and clinicians
and those of the managers who
ran the company. The therapists and clinicians evaluated
the company's success in terms
of its delivery of high-quality
health care. InSpeech manage-
ment, led by executives with financial services and ven-
ture capital backgrounds, measured the company's
worth exclusively in terms of financial success. Management's single-minded emphasis on increasing hours of
reimbursable care turned clinicians off. They took management's performance orientation for indifference to
patient care and left the company in droves.

At NovaCare,
executives defined
organizational
values and introduced
structural changes
to support those values.

CEO John Foster recognized the need for a common
frame of reference and a common language to unify the
diverse groups. So he brought in consultants to conduct
interviews and focus groups with the company's health
care professionals, managers, and customers. Based on
the results, an employee task force drafted a proposed
vision statement for the company, and another 250
employees suggested revisions. Then Foster and several
senior managers developed a succinct statement of the

company's guiding purpose and fundamental beliefs that could be used as a framework for making decisions and setting goals, policies, and practices.

Unlike a code of conduct, which articulates specific behavioral standards, the statement of vision, purposes, and beliefs lays out in very simple terms the company's central purpose and core values.

At NovaCare, clinicians took management's performance orientation for indifference to patient care and left the company in droves.

The purpose—meeting the rehabilitation needs of patients through clinical leadership—is supported by four key beliefs: respect for the individual, service to the customer, pursuit of excellence, and commitment to personal integrity. Each value is discussed with examples of how it is manifested in the day-to-day activities and policies of the company, such as how to measure the quality of care.

To support the newly defined values, the company changed its name to NovaCare and introduced a number of structural and operational changes. Field managers and clinicians were given greater decision-making authority; clinicians were provided with additional resources to assist in the delivery of effective therapy; and a new management structure integrated the various therapies offered by the company. The hiring of new corporate personnel with health care backgrounds reinforced the company's new clinical focus.

The introduction of the vision, purpose, and beliefs met with varied reactions from employees, ranging from cool skepticism to open enthusiasm. One employee remembered thinking the talk about values "much ado about nothing." Another recalled, "It was really wonderful. It gave us a goal that everyone aspired to, no matter what their place in the company." At first, some were baffled about how the vision, purpose, and beliefs were to be used. But, over time, managers became more adept at explaining and using them as a guide. When a customer tried to hire away a valued employee, for example, managers considered raiding the customer's company for employees. After reviewing the beliefs, the managers abandoned the idea.

NovaCare managers acknowledge and company surveys indicate that there is plenty of room for improvement. While the values are used as a firm reference point for decision making and evaluation in some areas of the company, they are still viewed with reservation in others. Some managers do not "walk the talk," employees complain. And recently acquired companies have yet to be fully integrated into the program. Nevertheless, many NovaCare employees say the values initiative played a critical role in the company's 1990 turnaround.

The values reorientation also helped the company deal with its most serious problem: turnover among health care providers. In 1990, the turnover rate stood at 32%, still above target but a significant improvement over the 1988 rate of 57%. By 1993, turnover had dropped to 27%. Moreover, recruiting new clinicians became easier. Barely able to hire 25 new clinicians each month in 1988, the company added 776 in 1990 and 2,546 in 1993. Indeed, one employee who left during the 1988 turmoil said that her decision to return in 1990 hinged on the company's adoption of the vision, purpose, and beliefs.

Wetherill Associates: Defining Right Action

Wetherill Associates, Inc.—a small, privately held supplier of electrical parts to the automotive market—has neither a conventional code of conduct nor a statement of values. Instead, WAI has a *Quality Assurance Manual*—a combination of philosophy text, conduct guide, technical manual, and company profile—that describes the company's commitment to honesty and its guiding principle of right action.

WAI doesn't have a corporate ethics officer who reports to top management, because at WAI, the company's corporate ethics officer *is* top management. Marie Bothe, WAI's chief executive officer, sees her main function as keeping the 350-employee company on the path of right action and looking for opportunities to help the community. She delegates the "technical" aspects of the business—marketing, finance, personnel, operations—to other members of the organization.

Right action, the basis for all of WAI's decisions, is a well-developed approach that challenges most conventional management thinking. The company explicitly rejects the usual conceptual boundaries that separate morality and self-interest. Instead, they define right behavior as logically, expediently, and morally right. Managers teach employees to look at the needs of the customers, suppliers, and the community—in addition to those of the company and its employees—when making decisions.

WAI also has a unique approach to competition. One employee explains, "We are not 'in competition' with anybody. We just do what we have to do to serve the customer." Indeed, when occasionally unable to fill orders, WAI salespeople refer customers to competitors. Artificial incentives, such as sales contests, are never used to spur individual performance. Nor are sales results used in determining compensation. Instead, the focus is on teamwork and customer service. Managers tell all new recruits that absolute honesty, mutual courtesy, and respect are standard operating procedure.

Newcomers generally react positively to company philosophy, but not all are prepared for such a radical departure from the practices they have known elsewhere. Recalling her initial interview, one recruit described her response to being told that lying was not allowed, "What do you mean? No lying? I'm a buyer. I lie for a living!" Today she is persuaded that the policy makes sound business sense. WAI is known for informing suppliers of overshipments as well as undershipments and for scrupulous honesty in the sale of parts, even when deception cannot be readily detected.

Since its entry into the distribution business 13 years ago, WAI has seen its revenues climb steadily from just under $1 million to nearly $98 million in 1993, and this in an industry with little growth. Once seen as an upstart beset by naysayers and industry skeptics, WAI is now credited with entering and professionalizing an industry in which kickbacks, bribes, and "gratuities" were commonplace. Employees—equal numbers of men and women ranging in age from 17 to 92—praise the work environment as both productive and supportive.

Creating an organization that encourages exemplary conduct may be the best way to prevent damaging misconduct.

WAI's approach could be difficult to introduce in a larger, more traditional organization. WAI is a small company founded by 34 people who shared a belief in right action; its ethical values were naturally built into the organization from the start. Those values are so deeply ingrained in the company's culture and operating systems that they have been largely self-sustaining. Still, the company has developed its own training program and takes special care to hire people willing to support right action. Ethics and job skills are considered equally important in determining an individual's competence and suitability for employment. For WAI, the challenge will be to sustain its vision as the company grows and taps into markets overseas.

At WAI, as at Martin Marietta and NovaCare, a management-led commitment to ethical values has contributed to competitiveness, positive workforce morale, as well as solid sustainable relationships with the company's key constituencies. In the end, creating a climate that encourages exemplary conduct may be the best way to discourage damaging misconduct. Only in such an environment do rogues really act alone.

Corporate Fines Under the Federal Sentencing Guidelines

WHAT SIZE FINE IS A CORPORATION likely to pay if convicted of a crime? It depends on a number of factors, some of which are beyond a CEO's control, such as the existence of a prior record of similar misconduct. But it also depends on more controllable factors. The most important of these are reporting and accepting responsibility for the crime, cooperating with authorities, and having an effective program in place to prevent and detect unlawful behavior.

The following example, based on a case studied by the United States Sentencing Commission, shows how the 1991 Federal Sentencing Guidelines have affected overall fine levels and how managers' actions influence organizational fines.

Acme Corporation was charged and convicted of mail fraud. The company systematically charged customers who damaged rented automobiles more than the actual cost of repairs. Acme also billed some customers for the cost of repairs to vehicles for which they were not responsible. Prior to the criminal adjudication, Acme paid $13.7 million in restitution to the customers who had been overcharged.

Deciding before the enactment of the sentencing guidelines, the judge in the criminal case imposed a fine of $6.85 million, roughly half the pecuniary loss suffered by Acme's customers. Under the sentencing guidelines, however, the results could have been dramatically different. Acme could have been fined anywhere from 5% to 200% the loss suffered by customers, depending on whether or not it had an effective program to prevent and detect violations of law and on whether or not it reported the crime, cooperated with authorities, and accepted responsibility for the unlawful conduct. If a high ranking official at Acme were found to have been involved, the maximum fine could have been as large as $54,800,000 or four times the loss to Acme customers. The following chart shows a possible range of fines for each situation:

What Fine Can Acme Expect?

	Maximum	Minimum
Program, reporting, cooperation, responsibility	$2,740,000	$685,000
Program only	10,960,000	5,480,000
No program, no reporting, no cooperation, no responsibility	27,400,000	13,700,000
No program, no reporting, no cooperation, no responsibility, involvement of high-level personnel	54,800,000	27,400,000

Source: Based on Case No.: 88-266, United States Sentencing Commission, *Supplementary Report on Sentencing Guidelines for Organizations.*

The Hallmarks of an Effective Integrity Strategy

THERE IS NO ONE RIGHT integrity strategy. Factors such as management personality, company history, culture, lines of business, and industry regulations must be taken into account when shaping an appropriate set of values and designing an implementation program. Still, several features are common to efforts that have achieved some success:

- *The guiding values and commitments make sense and are clearly communicated.* They reflect important organizational obligations and widely shared aspirations that appeal to the organization's members. Employees at all levels take them seriously, feel comfortable discussing them, and have a concrete understanding of their practical importance. This does not signal the absence of ambiguity and conflict but a willingness to seek solutions compatible with the framework of values.

- *Company leaders are personally committed, credible, and willing to take action on the values they espouse.* They are not mere mouthpieces. They are willing to scrutinize their own decisions. Consistency on the part of leadership is key. Waffling on values will lead to employee cynicism and a rejection of the program. At the same time, managers must assume responsibility for making tough calls when ethical obligations conflict.

- *The espoused values are integrated into the normal channels of management decision making and are reflected in the organization's critical activities:* the development of plans, the setting of goals, the search for opportunities, the allocation of resources, the gathering and communication of information, the measurement of performance, and the promotion and advancement of personnel.

- **The company's systems and structures support and reinforce its values.** Information systems, for example, are designed to provide timely and accurate information. Reporting relationships are structured to build in checks and balances to promote objective judgment. Performance appraisal is sensitive to means as well as ends.

- **Managers throughout the company have the decision-making skills, knowledge, and competencies needed to make ethically sound decisions on a day-to-day basis.** Ethical thinking and awareness must be part of every managers' mental equipment. Ethics education is usually part of the process.

Success in creating a climate for responsible and ethically sound behavior requires continuing effort and a considerable investment of time and resources. A glossy code of conduct, a high-ranking ethics officer, a training program, an annual ethics audit—these trappings of an ethics program do not necessarily add up to a responsible, law-abiding organization whose espoused values match its actions. A formal ethics program can serve as a catalyst and a support system, but organizational integrity depends on the integration of the company's values into its driving systems.

Originally published in March–April 1994
Reprint 94207

Values in Tension

Ethics Away from Home

THOMAS DONALDSON

Executive Summary

WHAT SHOULD MANAGERS working abroad do
when they encounter business practices that seem unethical? Should they, in the spirit of cultural relativism, tell
themselves to do in Rome as the Romans do? Or should
they take an absolutist approach, using the ethical standards they use at home no matter where they are?

According to Thomas Donaldson, the answer lies
somewhere in between. Some activities are wrong no
matter where they take place. Dumping pollutants for
unprotected workers to handle is one example of a practice that violates what Donaldson calls *core human values:* respect for human dignity, respect for basic rights,
and good citizenship. But some practices that are unethical in one part of the world might be ethical in another.
What may feel like bribery to an American, for example,
may be in keeping with Japan's longstanding tradition of

113

gift giving. And what may seem like inhumane wage rates to citizens of developed countries may be acceptable in developing countries that are trying to attract investment and improve standards of living.

Many business practices are neither black nor white but exist in a gray zone, a *moral free space* through which managers must navigate. Levi Strauss and Motorola have helped managers by treating company values as absolutes and insisting that suppliers and customers do the same. And, perhaps even more important, both companies have developed detailed codes of conduct that provide clear direction on ethical behavior but also leave room for managers to use the moral imagination that will allow them to resolve ethical tensions responsibly and creatively.

W HEN WE LEAVE HOME and cross our nation's boundaries, moral clarity often blurs. Without a backdrop of shared attitudes, and without familiar laws and judicial procedures that define standards of ethical conduct, certainty is elusive. Should a company invest in a foreign country where civil and political rights are violated? Should a company go along with a host country's discriminatory employment practices? If companies in developed countries shift facilities to developing nations that lack strict environmental and health regulations, or if those companies choose to fill management and other top-level positions in a host nation with people from the home country, whose standards should prevail?

Even the best-informed, best-intentioned executives must rethink their assumptions about business practice in foreign settings. What works in a company's home country can fail in a country with different standards of ethical conduct. Such difficulties are unavoidable for businesspeople who live and work abroad.

But how can managers resolve the problems? What are the principles that can help them work through the maze of cultural differences and establish codes of conduct for globally ethical business practice? How can companies answer the toughest question in global business ethics: What happens when a host country's ethical standards seem lower than the home country's?

Competing Answers

One answer is as old as philosophical discourse. According to cultural relativism, no culture's ethics are better than any other's; therefore there are no international rights and wrongs. If the people of Indonesia tolerate the bribery of their public officials, so what? Their attitude is no better or worse than that of people in Denmark or Singapore who refuse to offer or accept bribes. Likewise, if Belgians fail to find insider trading morally repugnant, who cares? Not enforcing insider-trading laws is no more or less ethical than enforcing such laws.

The cultural relativist's creed—When in Rome, do as the Romans do—is tempting, especially when failing to do as the locals do means forfeiting business opportunities. The inadequacy of cultural relativism, however, becomes apparent when the practices in question are more damaging than petty bribery or insider trading.

In the late 1980s, some European tanneries and pharmaceutical companies were looking for cheap waste-dumping sites. They approached virtually every country on Africa's west coast from Morocco to the Congo. Nigeria agreed to take highly toxic polychlorinated biphenyls.

Unprotected local workers, wearing thongs and shorts, unloaded barrels of PCBs and placed them near a residential area. Neither the residents nor the workers knew that the barrels contained toxic waste.

We may denounce governments that permit such abuses, but many countries are unable to police transnational corporations adequately even if they want to. And in many countries, the combination of ineffective enforcement and inadequate regulations leads to behavior by unscrupulous companies that is clearly wrong. A few years ago, for example, a group of investors became interested in restoring the SS *United States*, once a luxurious ocean liner. Before the actual restoration could begin, the ship had to be stripped of its asbestos lining. A bid from a U.S. company, based on U.S. standards for asbestos removal, priced the job at more than $100 million. A company in the Ukranian city of Sevastopol offered to do the work for less than $2 million. In October 1993, the ship was towed to Sevastopol.

A cultural relativist would have no problem with that outcome, but I do. A country has the right to establish its own health and safety regulations, but in the case described above, the standards and the terms of the contract could not possibly have protected workers in Sevastopol from known health risks. Even if the contract met Ukranian standards, ethical businesspeople must object. Cultural relativism is morally blind. There are fundamental values that cross cultures, and companies must uphold them. (For an economic argument against cultural relativism, see "The Culture and Ethics of Software Piracy" at the end of this article.)

At the other end of the spectrum from cultural relativism is ethical imperialism, which directs people to do everywhere exactly as they do at home. Again, an understandably appealing approach but one that is clearly inadequate. Consider the large U.S. computer-products company that in 1993 introduced a course on sexual harassment in its Saudi Arabian facility. Under the banner of global consistency, instructors used the same approach to train Saudi Arabian managers that they had used with U.S. managers: the participants were asked to discuss a case in which a manager makes sexually explicit remarks to a new female employee over drinks in a bar. The instructors failed to consider how the exercise would work in a culture with strict conventions governing relationships between men and women. As a result, the training sessions were ludicrous. They baffled and offended the Saudi participants, and the message to avoid coercion and sexual discrimination was lost.

The theory behind ethical imperialism is absolutism, which is based on three problematic principles. Absolutists believe that there is a single list of truths, that they can be expressed only with one set of concepts, and that they call for exactly the same behavior around the world.

The first claim clashes with many people's belief that different cultural traditions must be respected. In some cultures, loyalty to a community—family, organization, or society—is the foundation of all ethical behavior. The Japanese, for example, define business ethics in terms of loyalty to their companies, their business networks, and their nation. Americans place a higher value on liberty than on loyalty; the U.S. tradition of rights emphasizes equality, fairness, and individual freedom. It is hard to conclude that truth lies on one side or the other, but an absolutist would have us select just one.

The second problem with absolutism is the presumption that people must express moral truth using only one set of concepts. For instance, some absolutists insist that the language of basic rights provide the framework for any discussion of ethics. That means, though, that entire cultural traditions must be ignored. The notion of a right evolved with the rise of democracy in post-Renaissance Europe and the United States, but the term is not found in either Confucian or Buddhist traditions. We all learn ethics in the context of our particular cultures, and the power in the principles is deeply tied to the way in which they are expressed. Internationally accepted lists of moral principles, such as the United Nations' Universal Declaration of Human Rights, draw on many cultural and religious traditions. As philosopher Michael Walzer has noted, "There is no Esperanto of global ethics."

The third problem with absolutism is the belief in a global standard of ethical behavior. Context must shape ethical practice. Very low wages, for example, may be considered unethical in rich, advanced countries, but developing nations may be acting ethically if they encourage investment and improve living standards by accepting low wages. Likewise, when people are mal-nourished or starving, a government may be wise to use more fertilizer in order to improve crop yields, even though that means settling for relatively high levels of thermal water pollution.

When cultures have different standards of ethical behavior—and different ways of handling unethical behavior—a company that takes an absolutist approach may find itself making a disastrous mistake. When a manager at a large U.S. specialty-products company in China caught an employee stealing, she followed the company's practice and turned the employee over to the provincial authorities, who executed him. Managers can-not operate in another culture without being aware of that culture's attitudes toward ethics.

If companies can neither adopt a host country's ethics nor extend the home country's standards, what is the answer? Even the traditional litmus test—What would people think of your actions if they were written up on the front page of the newspaper?—is an unreliable guide, for there is no international consensus on standards of business conduct.

Balancing the Extremes: Three Guiding Principles

Companies must help managers distinguish between practices that are merely different and those that are wrong. For relativists, nothing is sacred and nothing is wrong. For absolutists, many things that are different are wrong. Neither extreme illuminates the real world of business decision making. The answer lies somewhere in between.

When it comes to shaping ethical behavior, companies must be guided by three principles.

- Respect for core human values, which determine the absolute moral threshold for all business activities.

- Respect for local traditions.

- The belief that context matters when deciding what is right and what is wrong.

Consider those principles in action. In Japan, people doing business together often exchange gifts—sometimes expensive ones—in keeping with long-standing Japanese tradition. When U.S. and European companies started doing a lot of business in Japan, many Western businesspeople thought that the practice of gift giving might be wrong rather than simply different. To them, accepting a gift felt like accepting a bribe. As Western companies have become more familiar with Japanese traditions, however, most have come to tolerate the practice and to set different limits on gift giving in Japan than they do elsewhere.

Respecting differences is a crucial ethical practice. Research shows that management ethics differ among cultures; respecting those differences means recognizing that some cultures have obvious weaknesses—as well as hidden strengths. Managers in Hong Kong, for example, have a higher tolerance for some forms of bribery than their Western counterparts, but they have a much lower tolerance for the failure to acknowledge a subordinate's work. In some parts of the Far East, stealing credit from a subordinate is nearly an unpardonable sin.

People often equate respect for local traditions with cultural relativism. That is incorrect. Some practices are clearly wrong. Union Carbide's tragic experience in Bhopal, India, provides one example. The company's executives seriously underestimated how much on-site management involvement was needed at the Bhopal plant to compensate for the country's poor infrastructure and regulatory capabilities. In the aftermath of the disastrous gas leak, the lesson is clear: companies using sophisticated technology in a developing country must evaluate that country's ability to oversee its safe use. Since the incident at Bhopal, Union Carbide has become a leader in advising companies on using hazardous technologies safely in developing countries.

Some activities are wrong no matter where they take place. But some practices that are unethical in one setting may be acceptable in another. For instance, the chemical EDB, a soil fungicide, is banned for use in the United States. In hot climates, however, it quickly becomes harmless through exposure to intense solar radiation and high soil temperatures. As long as the chemical is monitored, companies may be able to use EDB ethically in certain parts of the world.

Defining the Ethical Threshold: Core Values

Few ethical questions are easy for managers to answer. But there are some hard truths that must guide managers' actions, a set of what I call *core human values*, which define minimum ethical standards for all companies.[1] The right to good health and the right to economic advancement and an improved standard of living are two core human values. Another is what Westerners call the Golden Rule, which is recognizable in every major religious and ethical tradition around the world. In Book 15 of his *Analects*, for instance, Confucius counsels people to maintain reciprocity, or not to do to others what they do not want done to themselves.

Although no single list would satisfy every scholar, I believe it is possible to articulate three core values that incorporate the work of scores of theologians and philosophers around the world. To be broadly relevant, these values must include elements found in both Western and non-Western cultural and religious traditions. Consider the examples of values in the insert "What Do These Values Have in Common?"

At first glance, the values expressed in the two lists seem quite different. Nonetheless, in the spirit of what philosopher John Rawls calls *overlapping consensus*, one can see that the seemingly divergent values converge at key points. Despite important differences between Western and non-Western cultural and religious traditions, both express shared attitudes about what it means to be human. First, individuals must not treat others simply as tools; in other words, they must recognize a person's value as a human being. Next, individuals and communities must treat people in ways that respect people's basic rights. Finally, members of a community must work together to support and improve the institutions on which the community depends. I call those three values *respect for human dignity, respect for basic rights*, and *good citizenship*.

Those values must be the starting point for all companies as they formulate and evaluate standards of ethical conduct at home and abroad. But they are only a starting point. Companies need much more specific guidelines, and the first step to developing those is to translate the core human values into core values for business. What does it mean, for example, for a company to respect human dignity? How can a company be a good citizen?

I believe that companies can respect human dignity by creating and sustaining a corporate culture in which employees, customers, and suppliers are treated not as

What Do These Values Have in Common?

Non-Western	Western
Kyosei (Japanese): Living and working together for the common good.	Individual liberty
Dharma (Hindu): The fulfillment of inherited duty.	Egalitarianism
Santutthi (Buddhist): The importance of limited desires.	Political participation
Zakat (Muslim): The duty to give alms to the Muslim poor.	Human rights

means to an end but as people whose intrinsic value must be acknowledged, and by producing safe products and services in a safe workplace. Companies can respect basic rights by acting in ways that support and protect the individual rights of employees, customers, and surrounding communities, and by avoiding relationships that violate human beings' rights to health, education, safety, and an adequate standard of living. And companies can be good citizens by supporting essential social institutions, such as the economic system and the education system, and by working with host governments and other organizations to protect the environment.

The core values establish a moral compass for business practice. They can help companies identify practices that are acceptable and those that are intolerable—even if the practices are compatible with a host country's norms and laws. Dumping pollutants near people's homes and accepting inadequate standards for handling hazardous materials are two examples of actions that violate core values.

Similarly, if employing children prevents them from receiving a basic education, the practice is intolerable. Lying about product specifications in the act of selling may not affect human lives directly, but it too is intolerable because it violates the trust that is needed to sustain a corporate culture in which customers are respected.

Sometimes it is not a company's actions but those of a supplier or customer that pose problems. Take the case of the Tan family, a large supplier for Levi Strauss. The Tans were allegedly forcing 1,200 Chinese and Filipino women to work 74 hours per week in guarded compounds on the Mariana Islands. In 1992, after repeated warnings to the Tans, Levi Strauss broke off business relations with them.

Creating an Ethical Corporate Culture

The core values for business that I have enumerated can help companies begin to exercise ethical judgment and think about how to operate ethically in foreign cultures, but they are not specific enough to guide managers through actual ethical dilemmas. Levi Strauss relied on a written code of conduct when figuring out how to deal with the Tan family. The company's Global Sourcing and Operating Guidelines, formerly called the Business Partner Terms of Engagement, state that Levi Strauss will "seek to identify and utilize business partners who aspire as individuals and in the conduct of all their businesses to a set of ethical standards not incompatible with our own." Whenever intolerable business situations arise, managers should be guided by precise statements that spell out the behavior and operating practices that the company demands.

Many companies don't do anything with their codes of conduct; they simply paste them on the wall.

Ninety percent of all *Fortune* 500 companies have codes of conduct, and 70% have statements of vision and values. In Europe and the Far East, the percentages are lower but are increasing rapidly. Does that mean that most companies have what they need? Hardly. Even though most large U.S. companies have both statements of values and codes of conduct, many might be better off if they didn't. Too many companies don't do anything with the documents; they simply paste them on the wall to impress employees, customers, suppliers, and the public. As a result, the senior managers who drafted the statements lose credibility by proclaiming values and not living up to them. Companies such as Johnson & Johnson, Levi Strauss, Motorola, Texas Instruments, and Lockheed Martin, however, do a great deal to make the words meaningful. Johnson & Johnson, for example, has become well known for its Credo Challenge sessions, in which managers discuss ethics in the context of their current business problems and are invited to criticize the company's credo and make suggestions for changes. The participants' ideas are passed on to the company's senior managers. Lockheed Martin has created an innovative site on the World Wide Web and on its local network that gives employees, customers, and suppliers access to the company's ethical code and the chance to voice complaints.

Codes of conduct must provide clear direction about ethical behavior when the temptation to behave unethically is strongest. The pronouncement in a code of conduct that bribery is unacceptable is useless unless accompanied by guidelines for gift giving, payments to get goods through customs, and "requests" from intermediaries who are hired to ask for bribes.

Motorola's values are stated very simply as "How we will always act: [with] constant respect for people [and] uncompromising integrity." The company's code of conduct, however, is explicit about actual business practice. With respect to bribery, for example, the code states that the "funds and assets of Motorola shall not be used, directly or indirectly, for illegal payments of any kind." It is unambiguous about what sort of payment is illegal: "the payment of a bribe to a public official or the kickback of funds to an employee of a customer. . . ." The code goes on to prescribe specific procedures for handling commissions to intermediaries, issuing sales invoices, and disclosing confidential information in a sales transaction—all situations in which employees might have an opportunity to accept or offer bribes.

Codes of conduct must be explicit to be useful, but they must also leave room for a manager to use his or her judgment in situations requiring cultural sensitivity. Host-country employees shouldn't be forced to adopt all home-country values and renounce their own. Again, Motorola's code is exemplary. First, it gives clear direction: "Employees of Motorola will respect the laws, customs, and traditions of each country in which they operate, but will, at the same time, engage in no course of conduct which, even if legal, customary, and accepted in any such country, could be deemed to be in violation of the accepted business ethics of Motorola or the laws of the United States relating to business ethics." After laying down such absolutes, Motorola's code then makes clear when individual judgment will be necessary. For example, employees may sometimes accept certain kinds of small gifts "in rare circumstances, where the refusal to accept a gift" would injure Motorola's "legitimate business interests." Under certain circumstances, such gifts "may be accepted so long as the gift inures to the benefit of Motorola" and not "to the benefit of the Motorola employee."

Many activities are neither good nor bad but exist in moral free space.

Striking the appropriate balance between providing clear direction and leaving room for individual judgment makes crafting corporate values statements and ethics codes one of the hardest tasks that executives confront. The words are only a start. A company's leaders need to refer often to their organization's credo and code and must themselves be credible, committed, and consistent. If senior managers act as though ethics don't matter, the rest of the company's employees won't think they do, either.

Conflicts of Development and Conflicts of Tradition

Managers living and working abroad who are not prepared to grapple with moral ambiguity and tension should pack their bags and come home. The view that all business practices can be categorized as either ethical or unethical is too simple. As Einstein is reported to have said, "Things should be as simple as possible—but no simpler." Many business practices that are considered unethical in one setting may be ethical in another. Such activities are neither black nor white but exist in what Thomas Dunfee and I have called *moral free space.*[2] In this gray zone, there are no tight prescriptions for a company's behavior. Managers must chart their own courses—as long as they do not violate core human values.

Consider the following example. Some successful Indian companies offer employees the opportunity for one of their children to gain a job with the company once the child has completed a certain level in school. The companies honor this commitment even when other applicants are more qualified than an employee's child. The perk is extremely valuable in a country where jobs are hard to find, and it reflects the Indian culture's belief that the West has gone too far in allowing economic opportunities to break up families. Not surprisingly, the perk is among the most cherished by employees, but in most Western countries, it would be branded unacceptable nepotism. In the United States, for example, the ethical principle of equal opportunity holds that jobs should go to the applicants with the best qualifications. If a U.S. company made such promises to its employees, it would violate regulations established by the Equal Employment Opportunity Commission. Given this difference in ethical attitudes, how should U.S. managers react to Indian nepotism? Should they condemn the Indian companies, refusing to accept them as partners or suppliers until they agree to clean up their act?

Despite the obvious tension between nepotism and principles of equal opportunity, I cannot condemn the practice for Indians. In a country, such as India, that emphasizes clan and family relationships and has catastrophic levels of unemployment, the practice must be viewed in moral free space. The decision to allow a special perk for employees and their children is not necessarily wrong—at least for members of that country.

How can managers discover the limits of moral free space? That is, how can they learn to distinguish a value in tension with their own from one that is intolerable? Helping managers develop good ethical judgment requires companies to be clear about their core values and codes of conduct. But even the most explicit set of guidelines cannot always provide answers. That is especially true in the thorniest ethical dilemmas, in which the host country's ethical standards not only are different but also seem lower than the home country's. Managers must recognize that when countries have different ethical standards, there are two types of conflict that commonly arise. Each type requires its own line of reasoning.

In the first type of conflict, which I call a *conflict of relative development*, ethical standards conflict because of the countries' different levels of economic development. As mentioned before, developing countries may accept wage rates that seem inhumane to more advanced countries in order to attract investment. As economic conditions in a developing country improve, the incidence of that sort of conflict usually decreases. The second type of conflict is a *conflict of cultural tradition*. For example, Saudi Arabia, unlike most other countries, does not allow women to serve as corporate managers. Instead, women may work in only a few professions, such as education and health care. The prohibition stems from strongly held religious and cultural beliefs; any increase in the country's level of economic development, which is already quite high, is not likely to change the rules.

To resolve a conflict of relative development, a manager must ask the following question: Would the practice be acceptable at home if my country were in a similar stage of economic development? Consider the difference between wage and safety standards in the United States and in Angola, where citizens accept lower standards on both counts. If a U.S. oil company is hiring Angolans to work on an offshore Angolan oil rig, can the company pay them lower wages than it pays U.S. workers in the Gulf of Mexico? Reasonable people have to answer yes if the alternative for Angola is the loss of both the foreign investment and the jobs.

Consider, too, differences in regulatory environments. In the 1980s, the government of India fought hard to be able to import Ciba-Geigy's Entero Vioform, a drug known to be enormously effective in fighting dysentery but one that had been banned in the United States because some users experienced side effects. Although dysentery was not a big problem in the United States, in India, poor public sanitation was contributing to epidemic levels of the disease. Was it unethical to make the drug available in India after it had been banned in the United States? On the contrary, rational people should consider it unethical not to do so. Apply our test: Would the United States, at an earlier stage of development, have used this drug despite its side effects? The answer is clearly yes.

But there are many instances when the answer to similar questions is no. Sometimes a host country's standards are inadequate at any level of economic devel-

If a company declared all gift giving unethical, it wouldn't be able to do business in Japan.

opment. If a country's pollution standards are so low that working on an oil rig would considerably increase a person's risk of developing cancer, foreign oil companies must refuse to do business there. Likewise, if the dangerous side effects of a drug treatment outweigh its benefits, managers should not accept health standards that ignore the risks.

When relative economic conditions do not drive tensions, there is a more objective test for resolving ethical problems. Managers should deem a practice permissible only if they can answer no to both of the following questions: Is it possible to conduct business successfully in the host country without undertaking the practice? and Is the practice a violation of a core human value? Japanese gift giving is a perfect example of a conflict of cultural tradition. Most experienced businesspeople, Japanese and non-Japanese alike, would agree that doing business in Japan would be virtually impossible without adopting the practice. Does gift giving violate a core human value? I cannot identify one that it violates. As a result, gift giving may be permissible for foreign companies in Japan even if it conflicts with ethical attitudes at home. In fact, that conclusion is widely accepted, even by companies such as Texas Instruments and IBM, which are outspoken against bribery.

Does it follow that all nonmonetary gifts are acceptable or that bribes are generally acceptable in countries
where they are common? Not at all. (See "The Problem
with Bribery" at the end of this article.) What makes the
routine practice of gift giving acceptable in Japan are the
limits in its scope and intention. When gift giving moves
outside those limits, it soon collides with core human
values. For example, when Carl Kotchian, president of
Lockheed in the 1970s, carried suitcases full of cash to
Japanese politicians, he went beyond the norms established by Japanese tradition. That incident galvanized
opinion in the United States Congress and helped lead to
passage of the Foreign Corrupt Practices Act. Likewise,
Roh Tae Woo went beyond the norms established by
Korean cultural tradition when he accepted $635.4 mil-
lion in bribes as president of the Republic of Korea
between 1988 and 1993.

Guidelines for Ethical Leadership

Learning to spot intolerable practices and to exercise
good judgment when ethical conflicts arise requires
practice. Creating a company culture that rewards ethical behavior is essential. The following guidelines for
developing a global ethical perspective among managers
can help.

**Treat corporate values and formal standards of
conduct as absolutes.** Whatever ethical standards a
company chooses, it cannot waver on its principles
either at home or abroad. Consider what has become
part of company lore at Motorola. Around 1950, a
senior executive was negotiating with officials of a
South American government on a $10 million sale

that would have increased the company's annual net profits by nearly 25%. As the negotiations neared completion, however, the executive walked away from the deal because the officials were asking for $1 million for "fees." CEO Robert Galvin not only supported the executive's decision but also made it clear that Motorola would neither accept the sale on any terms nor do business with those government officials again. Retold over the decades, this story demonstrating Galvin's resolve has helped cement a culture of ethics for thousands of employees at Motorola.

Design and implement conditions of engagement for suppliers and customers. Will your company do business with any customer or supplier? What if a customer or supplier uses child labor? What if it has strong links with organized crime? What if it pressures your company to break a host country's laws? Such issues are best not left for spur-of-the-moment decisions. Some companies have realized that. Sears, for instance, has developed a policy of not contracting production to companies that use prison labor or infringe on workers' rights to health and safety. And BankAmerica has specified as a condition for many of its loans to developing countries that environmental standards and human rights must be observed.

Allow foreign business units to help formulate ethical standards and interpret ethical issues. The French pharmaceutical company Rhône-Poulenc Rorer has allowed foreign subsidiaries to augment lists of corporate ethical principles with their own suggestions. Texas Instruments has paid special attention to issues of international business ethics by creating the Global Business Practices Council, which is made up of managers from countries in which the company operates. With the overarching intent to create a "global ethics strategy, locally deployed," the council's mandate is to provide ethics education and create local processes that will help managers in the company's foreign business units resolve ethical conflicts.

In host countries, support efforts to decrease institutional corruption. Individual managers will not be able to wipe out corruption in a host country, no matter how many bribes they turn down. When a host country's tax system, import and export procedures, and procurement practices favor unethical players, companies must take action.

Many companies have begun to participate in reforming host-country institutions. General Electric, for example, has taken a strong stand in India, using the media to make repeated condemnations of bribery in business and government. General Electric and others have found, however, that a single company usually cannot drive out entrenched corruption. Transparency International, an organization based in Germany, has been effective in helping coalitions of companies, government officials, and others work to reform bribery-ridden bureaucracies in Russia, Bangladesh, and elsewhere.

Exercise moral imagination. Using moral imagination means resolving tensions responsibly and creatively. Coca-Cola, for instance, has consistently turned down requests for bribes from Egyptian officials but has managed to gain political support and public trust by sponsoring a project to plant fruit trees. And take the example of Levi Strauss, which discovered in the early 1990s that two of its suppliers in Bangladesh were employing children under the age of 14—a practice that violated the company's principles but was tolerated in Bangladesh. Forcing the suppliers to fire the children would not have ensured that the children received an education, and it would have caused serious hardship for the families depending on the children's wages. In a creative arrangement, the suppliers agreed to pay the children's regular wages while they attended school and to offer each child a job at age 14. Levi Strauss, in turn, agreed to pay the children's tuition and provide books and uniforms. That arrangement allowed Levi Strauss to uphold its principles and provide long-term benefits to its host country.

Many people think of values as soft; to some they are usually unspoken. A South Seas island society uses the word *mokita,* which means, "the truth that everybody knows but nobody speaks." However difficult they are to articulate, values affect how we all behave. In a global business environment, values in tension are the rule rather than the exception. Without a company's commitment, statements of values and codes of ethics end up as empty platitudes that provide managers with no foundation for behaving ethically. Employees need and deserve more, and responsible members of the global business community can set examples for others to follow. The dark consequences of incidents such as Union Carbide's disaster in Bhopal remind us how high the stakes can be.

The Culture and Ethics of Software Piracy

BEFORE JUMPING ON THE cultural relativism bandwagon, stop and consider the potential economic consequences of a when-in-Rome attitude toward business ethics. Take a look at the current statistics on software piracy: In the United States, pirated software is estimated to be 35% of the total software market, and industry losses are estimated at $2.3 billion per year. The piracy rate is 57% in Germany and 80% in Italy and Japan; the rates in most Asian countries are estimated to be nearly 100%.

There are similar laws against software piracy in those countries. What, then, accounts for the differences? Although a country's level of economic development plays a large part, culture, including ethical attitudes, may be a more crucial factor. The 1995 annual report of the Software Publishers Association connects software piracy directly to culture and attitude. It describes Italy and Hong Kong as having "'first world' per capita incomes, along with 'third world' rates of piracy." When asked whether one should use software without paying for it, most people, including people in Italy and Hong Kong, say no. But people in some countries regard the practice as *less* unethical than people in other countries do. Confucian culture, for example, stresses that individuals should share what they create with society. That may be, in part, what prompts the Chinese and other Asians to view the concept of intellectual property as a means for the West to monopolize its technological superiority.

What happens if ethical attitudes around the world permit large-scale software piracy? Software companies won't want to invest as much in developing new products, because they cannot expect any return on their investment in certain parts of the world. When ethics fail to support technological creativity, there are consequences that go beyond statistics—jobs are lost and livelihoods jeopardized.

Companies must do more than lobby foreign governments for tougher enforcement of piracy laws. They must cooperate with other companies and with local organizations to help citizens understand the consequences of piracy and to encourage the evolution of a different ethic toward the practice.

The Problem with Bribery

BRIBERY IS WIDESPREAD and insidious. Managers in transnational companies routinely confront bribery even though most countries have laws against it. The fact is that officials in many developing countries wink at the practice, and the salaries of local bureaucrats are so low that many consider bribes a form of remuneration. The U.S. Foreign Corrupt Practices Act defines allowable limits on petty bribery in the form of routine payments required to move goods through customs. But demands for bribes often exceed those limits, and there is seldom a good solution.

Bribery disrupts distribution channels when goods languish on docks until local handlers are paid off, and it destroys incentives to compete on quality and cost when purchasing decisions are based on who pays what under the table. Refusing to acquiesce is often tantamount to giving business to unscrupulous companies.

I believe that even routine bribery is intolerable. Bribery undermines market efficiency and predictability, thus ultimately denying people their right to a minimal standard of living. Some degree of ethical commitment—some sense that everyone will play by the rules—is necessary for a sound economy. Without an ability to predict outcomes, who would be willing to invest?

There was a U.S. company whose shipping crates were regularly pilfered by handlers on the docks of Rio de Janeiro. The handlers would take about 10% of the contents of the crates, but the company was never sure which 10% it would be. In a partial solution, the company began sending two crates—the first with 90% of the merchandise, the second with 10%. The handlers learned to take the second crate and leave the first untouched. From the company's perspective, at least knowing which goods it would lose was an improvement.

Bribery does more than destroy predictability; it undermines essential social and economic systems. That truth is not lost on businesspeople in countries where the practice is woven into the social fabric. CEOs in India admit that their companies engage constantly in bribery, and they say that they have considerable disgust for the practice. They blame government policies in part, but Indian executives also know that their country's business practices perpetuate corrupt behavior. Anyone walking the streets of Calcutta, where it is clear that even a dramatic redistribution of wealth would still leave most of India's inhabitants in dire poverty, comes face-to-face with the devastating effects of corruption.

Notes

1. In other writings, Thomas W. Dunfee and I have used the term *hypernorm* instead of *core human value*.

2. Thomas Donaldson and Thomas W. Dunfee, "Toward a Unified Conception of Business Ethics: Integrative Social

Contracts Theory," *Academy of Management Review*, April 1994; and "Integrative Social Contracts Theory: A Communitarian Conception of Economic Ethics," *Economics and Philosophy*, spring 1995.

Originally published in September–October 1996
Reprint 96502

The Discipline of
Building Character

JOSEPH L. BADARACCO, JR.

Executive Summary

WHAT IS THE DIFFERENCE between an ethical decision and what the author calls a *defining moment?* An ethical decision typically involves choosing between two options: one we know to be right and another we know to be wrong. A defining moment challenges us in a deeper way by asking us to choose between two or more ideals in which we deeply believe. Such decisions rarely have one "correct" response. Taken cumulatively over many years, they form the basis of an individual's character.

Defining moments ask executives to dig below the busy surface of their lives and refocus on their core values and principles. Once uncovered, those values and principles renew their senses of purpose at the workplace and act as a springboard for shrewd, pragmatic, politically astute action. Three types of defining moments are particularly common in today's workplace. The first type is largely an issue of personal identity. It raises the question, Who am I? The second type concerns groups as well as individuals. It raises the question, Who are we? The third kind involves defining as company's role within society. It raises the question, Who is the company?

By learning to identify each of those three situations, managers can learn to navigate right-versus-right decisions successfully. The author asks a series of practical questions that will help managers take time out to examine their values and then transform their beliefs into action. By engaging in this process of self-inquiry, managers will be gaining the tools to tackle their most elusive, challenging, and essential business dilemmas.

W E HAVE ALL EXPERIENCED, at one time or another, situations in which our professional responsibilities unexpectedly come into conflict with our deepest values. A budget crisis forces us to dismiss a loyal, hardworking employee. Our daughter has a piano recital on the same afternoon that our biggest client is scheduled to visit our office. At these times, we are caught in a conflict between right and right. And no matter which option we choose, we feel like we've come up short.

Managers respond to these situations in a variety of ways: some impulsively "go with their gut"; others talk it over with their friends, colleagues, or families; still others think back to what a mentor would do in similar circumstances. In every case, regardless of what path is chosen, these decisions taken cumulatively over many years form the very basis of an individual's character. For that reason, I call them *defining moments*.

What is the difference between a tough ethical decision and a defining moment? An ethical decision typically involves choosing between two options: one we know to be right and another we know to be wrong. A defining moment, however, challenges us in a deeper way by asking us to choose between two or more ideals in which we deeply believe. Such challenges rarely have a "correct" response. Rather, they are situations created by circumstance that ask us to step forward and, in the words of the American philosopher John Dewey, "form, reveal, and test" ourselves. We form our character in defining moments because we commit to irreversible courses of action that shape our personal and professional identities. We reveal something new about us to ourselves and others because defining moments uncover something that had been hidden or crystallize something that had been only partially known. And we test ourselves because we discover whether we will live up to our personal ideals or only pay them lip service.

As I have interviewed and studied business leaders, I have found that the ones who are most satisfied with the way they resolve their defining moments possess skills that are left off most job descriptions. Specifically, they are able to take time out from the chain of managerial tasks that consumes their time and undertake a process of probing self-inquiry—a process that is more often carried out on the run rather than in quiet seclusion. They are able to dig below the busy surface of their daily lives and refocus on their core values and principles. Once uncovered, those values and principles renew their sense of purpose at work and act as a

To become leaders, managers need to translate their personal values into calculated action.

springboard for shrewd, pragmatic, politically astute action. By repeating this process again and again throughout their work lives, these executives are able to craft an authentic and strong identity based on their own, rather than on someone else's, understanding of what is right. And in this way, they begin to make the transition from being a manager to becoming a leader.

But how can an executive trained in the practical, extroverted art of management learn to engage in such an intuitive, personal process of introspection? In this article, I will describe a series of down-to-earth questions that will help managers take time out from the hustle and bustle of the workplace. These practical, thought-provoking questions are designed to transform values and beliefs into calculated action. They have been drawn from well-known classic and contemporary philosophers but remain profound and flexible enough to embrace a wide range of contemporary right-versus-right decisions. By taking time out to engage in this process of self-inquiry, managers will by no means be conducting a fruitless exercise in escapism; rather, they will be getting a better handle on their most elusive, challenging, and essential business problems.

In today's workplace, three kinds of defining moments are particularly common. The first type is largely an issue of personal identity. It raises the question, Who am I? The second type is organizational as well as personal: both the character of groups within an organization and the character of an individual manager are at stake. It raises the question, Who are we? The third type of defining moment is the most complex and involves defining a company's role in society. It raises the question, Who is the company? By learning to identify each of these three defining moments, managers will learn to navigate right-versus-right decisions with grace and strength. (See "A Guide to Defining Moments" for more information.)

Who am I? Defining Moments for Individuals

The most basic type of defining moment demands that managers resolve an urgent issue of personal identity that has serious implications for their careers. Two "rights" present themselves, each one representing a plausible and usually attractive life choice. And therein lies the problem: there is no one right answer; right is set against right.

CONFLICTING FEELINGS

When caught in this bind, managers can begin by taking a step back and looking at the conflict not as a problem but as a natural tension between two valid perspectives. To flesh out this tension, we can ask, *What feelings and intuitions are coming into conflict in this situation?* As Aristotle discussed in his classic work *Ethics*, people's feelings can actually help them make sense of an issue, understand its basic dimensions, and indicate what the stakes really are. In other words, our feelings and intuitions are both a form of intelligence and a source of insight.

Consider, for example, the case of a young analyst—we will call him Steve Lewis—who worked for a well-known investment bank in Manhattan.[1] Early one morning, Lewis, an African-American, found a message on his desk asking if he could fly to St. Louis in two days to help with a presentation to an important prospective client.

A Guide to Defining Moments

For Individuals

Who am I?

1. What feelings and intuitions are coming into conflict in this situation?

2. Which of the values that are in conflict are most deeply rooted in my life?

3. What combination of expediency and shrewdness, coupled with imagination and boldness, will help me implement my personal understanding of what is right?

For Managers of Work Groups

Who are we?

1. What are the other strong, persuasive interpretations of the ethics of this situation?

2. What point of view is most likely to win a contest of interpretations inside my organization and influence the thinking of other people?

3. Have I orchestrated a process that can make manifest the values I care about in my organization?

For Company Executives

Who is the company?

1. Have I done all I can to secure my position and the strength of my organization?

2. Have I thought creatively and boldly about my organization's role in society and its relationship to stockholders?

3. What combination of shrewdness, creativity, and tenacity will help me transform my vision into a reality?

The message came as a surprise to him. Lewis's company had a clear policy against including analysts in presentations or client meetings. Lewis, in fact, knew little about the subject of the St. Louis meeting, which concerned a specialized area of municipal finance. He was especially surprised to learn that he had been selected over more senior people in the public finance group.

Lewis immediately walked down the hall into the office of his friend and mentor, also an African-American, and asked him if he knew about the situation. His friend, a partner at the company, replied, "Let me tell you what's happening, Steve. Look at you and me. What do we have in common? Did you know that the new state treasurer of Missouri is also black? I hate for you to be introduced to this side of the business so soon, but the state treasurer wants to see at least one black professional at the meeting or else the company has no chance of being named a manager for this deal."

What if at this point Lewis were to step back and reframe the situation in terms of his feelings and intuitions? On the one hand, Lewis believed firmly that in order to maintain his self-respect, he had to earn his advancement at the company—and elsewhere in life. He was not satisfied to move up the ladder of success based on affirmative action programs or being a "token" member of the company. For that reason, he had always wanted to demonstrate through his work that he deserved his position. On the other hand, as a former athlete, Lewis had always prided himself on being a team player and did not believe in letting his teammates down. By examining his feelings and intuitions about the situation, Lewis learned that the issue at hand was more complex than whether or not to go to the presentation. It involved a conflict between two of his most deeply held beliefs.

DEEPLY ROOTED VALUES

By framing defining moments in terms of our feelings
and intuitions, we can remove the conflict from its business context and bring it to a more personal, and
manageable, level. Then we
To resolve their toughest   can consider a second ques-
business challenges,   tion to help resolve the con-
executives need to refocus   flict: *Which of the responsi-*
on their core values.   *bilities and values that are*
in conflict are most deeply
rooted in my life and in the communities I care about?
Tracing the roots of our values means understanding
their origins and evolution over time. It involves an effort
to understand which values and commitments really
mean the most to us.

Let's apply that approach to the case of Steve Lewis.
On the one hand, he had no doubt that he wanted to
become a partner at a major investment bank and that
he wanted to earn that position based on merit. Since his
sophomore year of college, Lewis had been drawn to the
idea of a career on Wall Street, and he had worked hard
and purposefully to make that idea a reality. When he
accepted his current job, he had finally set foot on the
path he had dreamed of, and neither the long hours nor
the detailed "grunt" work that was the lot of first-year
analysts gave him misgivings about his choice. He
believed he was pursuing his own values by seeking a
successful career at a Wall Street investment bank. It
was the kind of life he wanted to live and the kind of
work he enjoyed doing.

On the other hand, when Lewis considered his
African-American background, he thought about what
his parents had taught him. One episode from the early

1960s stood out in particular. His parents made a reservation at a restaurant that reputedly did not serve blacks. When they arrived, the hostess told them there had been a mistake. The reservation was lost, and they could not be seated. The restaurant was half empty. Lewis's parents turned around and left. When they got home, his mother made a new reservation under her maiden name. (His father had been a popular local athlete, whose name was widely recognized.) The restaurant suspected nothing. When they returned an hour later, the hostess, though hardly overjoyed, proceeded to seat them.

Lewis was still moved by the memory of what his parents had done, even as he sat in his office on Wall Street many years later. With his parents' example in mind, Lewis could begin to sense what seemed to be the best answer to his present dilemma. He would look at the situation as his parents' son. He would view it as an African-American, not as just another young investment banker. Lewis decided that he could not go to the meeting as the "token black." To do so would repudiate his parents' example. He decided, in effect, that his race was a vital part of his moral identity, one with a deeper and stronger relation to his core self than the professional role he had recently assumed.

Self-inquiry must lead to shrewd, persuasive, and self-confident action if it is to be an effective tool.

SHREWDNESS AND EXPEDIENCY

Introspection of the kind Steve Lewis engaged in can easily become divorced from real-world demands. We have all seen managers who unthinkingly throw themselves into a deeply felt personal cause and suffer serious personal and career setbacks. As the Renaissance philosopher Niccolò Machiavelli and other ethical pragmatists remind us, idealism untempered by realism often does little to improve the world. Hence, the next critical question becomes, *What combination of shrewdness and expediency, coupled with imagination and boldness, will help me implement my personal understanding of what is right?* This is, of course, a different question altogether from What should I do? It acknowledges that the business world is a bottom-line, rough-and-tumble arena where introspection alone won't get the job done. The process of looking inward must culminate in concrete action characterized by tenacity, persuasiveness, shrewdness, and self-confidence.

How did Lewis combine idealism with realism? He decided that he would join the presentation team, but he also gambled that he could do so on terms that were at least acceptable to him. He told the partner in charge, Bruce Anderson, that he felt honored to be asked to participate but added that he wanted to play a role in the presentation. He said he was willing to spend every minute of the next 30 hours in preparation. When Anderson asked why, Lewis said only that he wanted to earn his place on the team. Anderson reluctantly agreed. There was, it turned out, a minor element of the presentation that required the application of some basic analytical techniques with which Lewis was familiar. Lewis worked hard on the presentation, but when he stood up during the meeting for the 12 minutes allotted him, he had a terrible headache and wished he had refused Anderson's offer. His single day of cramming was no substitute for the weeks his colleagues had invested in the project. Nevertheless, his portion of the presentation went well, and he received praise from his colleagues for the work he had done.

On balance, Lewis had soundly defined the dilemma he faced and had taken an active role in solving it—he did not attend the meeting as a showpiece. At the same time, he may have strengthened his career prospects. He felt he had passed a minor test, a rite of passage at his company, and had demonstrated not only that he was willing to do what it took to get the job done but also that he would not be treated as a token member of the group. The white analysts and associates who were passed over probably grumbled a bit; but Lewis suspected that, if they had been dealt his hand, they would have played their cards as he did.

Who Are We? Defining Moments for Work Groups

As managers move up in an organization, defining moments become more difficult to resolve. In addition to looking at the situation as a conflict between two personal beliefs, managers must add another dimension: the values of their work group and their responsibilities to the people they manage. How, for example, should a manager respond to an employee who repeatedly shows up for work with the smell of alcohol on his breath? How should a manager respond to one employee who has made sexually suggestive remarks to another? In this type of defining moment, the problem and its resolution unfold not only as a personal drama within one's self but also as a drama among a group of people who work together. The issue becomes public and is important enough to define a group's future and shape its values.

POINTS OF VIEW

Many managers suffer from a kind of ethical myopia, believing that their entire group views a situation through the same lens that they do. This way of thinking rarely succeeds in bringing people together to accomplish common goals. Differences in upbringing, religion, ethnicity, and education make it difficult for any two people to view a situation similarly—let alone an entire group of people. The ethical challenge for a manager is not to impose his or her understanding of what is right on the group but to understand how other members view the dilemma. The manager must ask, *What are the other strong, persuasive interpretations of the ethics of this situation?*

A classic example of this kind of problem involved a 35-year-old manager, Peter Adario. Adario headed the marketing department of Sayer Microworld, a distributor of computer products. He was married and had three children. He had spent most of his career as a successful salesman and branch manager, and he eagerly accepted his present position because of its varied challenges. Three senior managers reporting to Adario supervised the other 50 employees in the marketing department, and Adario in turn reported to one of four vice presidents at corporate headquarters.

Adario had recently hired an account manager, Kathryn McNeil, who was a single mother. Although she was highly qualified and competent, McNeil was having a hard time keeping up with her work because of the time she needed to spend with her son. The pace at work was demanding: the company was in the middle of finishing a merger, and 60-hour work weeks had become the norm. McNeil was also having difficulty getting along with her supervisor, Lisa Walters, a midlevel manager in the department who reported to Adario. Walters was an ambitious, hard-driving woman who was excelling in Sayer Microworld's fast-paced environment. She was irritated by McNeil's chronic lateness and unpredictable work schedule. Adario had not paid much attention to Walters' concerns until the morning he found a handwritten note from her on top of his pile of unfinished paperwork. It was her second note to him in as many weeks. Both notes complained about McNeil's hours and requested that she be fired.

For Adario, who was himself a father and sympathetic to McNeil's plight, the situation was clearly a defining moment, pitting his belief that his employees needed time with their families against his duty to the department's bottom line. Adario decided to set up a meeting. He was confident that if he sat down with the two women the issue could somehow be resolved. Shortly before the meeting was to begin, however, Adario was stunned to learn that Walters had gone over his head and discussed the issue with one of the company's senior executives. The two then had gone to McNeil's office and had fired her. A colleague later told him that McNeil had been given four hours to pack her things and leave the premises.

Managers need to determine if their ethical vision will be supported by their coworkers and employees.

Where Adario saw right versus right, Walters saw right versus wrong. She believed that the basic ethical issue was McNeil's irresponsibility in not pulling her weight and Adario's lack of action on the issue. McNeil's customer account was crucial, and it was falling behind schedule during a period of near-crisis at the company.

Walters also believed that it was unfair for one member
of the badly overburdened team to receive special treatment. In retrospect, Adario could see that he and Walters looked at the same facts about McNeil and reached
very different conclusions. Had he recognized earlier that
his view was just one interpretation among many, he
might have realized that he was engaged in a difficult
contest of interpretations.

INFLUENCING BEHAVIOR

Identifying competing interpretations, of course, is only
part of the battle. Managers also need to take a hard look
at the organization in which they work and make a realistic assessment of whose interpretation will win out in
the end. A number of factors can determine which interpretation will prevail: company culture, group norms,
corporate goals and company policy, and the inevitable
political jockeying and battling inside organizations. In
the words of the American philosopher William James,
"The final victorious way of looking at things will be the
most completely impressive to the normal run of minds."
Therefore, managers need to ask themselves, *What point
of view is most likely to win the contest of interpretations
and influence the thinking and behavior of other people?*

Peter Adario would have benefited from mulling over
this question. If he had done so, he might have seen the
issue in terms of a larger work-family issue within the
company. For Adario and McNeil, the demands of work
and family meant constant fatigue, a sense of being
pulled in a thousand directions, and the frustration of
never catching up on all they had to do. To the other
employees at Sayer Microworld, most of whom were
young and not yet parents, the work-family conflict

meant that they sometimes had to work longer hours because other employees had families to attend to. Given the heavy workloads they were carrying, these single employees had little sympathy for Adario's family-oriented values.

TRUTH AS PROCESS

Planning ahead is at the heart of managerial work. One needs to learn to spot problems before they blow up into crises. The same is true for defining moments in groups. They should be seen as part of a larger process that, like any other, needs to be managed. Effective managers put into place the conditions for the successful resolution of defining moments long before those moments actually present themselves. For in the words of William James, "The truth of an idea is not a stagnant property inherent in it. Truth happens to an idea. It becomes true, is made true by events. Its verity is in fact an event, a process." Managers can start creating the conditions for a particular interpretation to prevail by asking, *Have I orchestrated a process that can make my interpretation win in my group?*

Adario missed subtle signals that a process opposed to his own had been under way for some time. Recall that Walters had sent Adario two notes, each suggesting that McNeil be replaced. What were those notes actually about? Were they tentative announcements of Walters's plans or tests of Adario's authority? And what did Walters make of Adario's failure to respond? She apparently interpreted his reaction—or lack thereof—as an indication that he would not stand in the way of firing McNeil. Walters may even have thought that Adario wanted McNeil fired but was unwilling to do it himself. In short,

Adario's defining moment had gone badly because Walters presented a compelling story to the company's top management; she thereby preempted Adario and filled the vacuum that he had created through his inaction.

Instead of waiting for the issue of work versus family to arise and take the group by surprise, Adario could have anticipated the problem and taken a proactive approach to defining a work culture that valued both family and work. Adario had ample opportunity to prevent the final turn of events from occurring. He could have promoted McNeil to others inside the company. In particular, he needed to emphasize the skills and experience, especially in account management, that she brought to the company. He also could have created opportunities for people to get to know McNeil personally, even to meet her son, so that they would understand and appreciate what she was accomplishing.

Some of the most challenging defining moments faced by managers ask them to balance work and family.

PLAYING TO WIN

One of the hallmarks of a defining moment is that there is a lot at stake for all the players in the drama. More often than not, the players will put their own interests first. In this type of business setting, neither the most well-meaning intentions nor the best-designed process will get the job done. Managers must be ready to roll up their sleeves and dive into the organizational fray, putting to use appropriate and effective tactics that will make their vision a reality. They need to reflect on the question, *Am I just playing along or am I playing to win?*

At Sayer Microworld, the contest of interpretations between Walters and Adario was clearly part of a larger power struggle. If Walters didn't have her eye on Adario's job before McNeil was fired, she probably did afterward: top management seemed to like her take-charge style. Whereas Adario was lobbing underhand softball pitches, Walters was playing hardball. At Sayer Microworld, do-the-right-thing idealism without organizational savvy was the sure path to obscurity. Adario's heart was in the right place when he hired McNeil. He believed she could do the job, he admired her courage, and he wanted to create a workplace in which she could flourish. But his praiseworthy intentions needed to be backed by a knack for maneuvering, shrewdness, and political savvy. Instead, Walters seized the moment. She timed her moves carefully and found a powerful ally in the senior manager who helped her carry out her plan.

Although Adario stumbled, it is worth noting that this defining moment taught him a great deal. In following up on McNeil's firing, Adario learned through the grapevine that many other employees shared his view of the work-family dilemma, and he began acting with more confidence than he had before. He told his boss that he disagreed with the decision to fire McNeil and objected strongly to the way the decision had been made. He then told Walters that her behavior would be noted in the next performance review he put in her file. Neither Walters nor the vice president said very much in response, and the issue never came up again. Adario had staked his claim, albeit belatedly. He had learned, in the words of Machiavelli,

To succeed, top-level executives must negotiate their ethical vision with shareholders, customers, and employees.

that "a man who has no position in society cannot even get a dog to bark at him."

Who Is the Company? Defining Moments for Executives

Redefining the direction of one's own life and the direction of one's work group requires a thoughtful blend of personal introspection and calculated action. But the men and women charged with running entire companies sometimes face an even more complex type of defining moment. They are asked to make manifest their understanding of what is right on a large stage—one that can include labor unions, the media, shareholders, and many other company stakeholders. Consider the complexity of the dilemma faced by a CEO who has just received a report of package tampering in one of the company's over-the-counter medications. Or consider the position of an executive who needs to formulate a response to reports in the media that women and children are being treated unfairly in the company's foreign plant. These types of decisions force top-level managers to commit not just themselves or their work groups but their entire company to an irreversible course of action.

PERSONAL AND ORGANIZATIONAL STRENGTH

In the face of such overwhelming decisions, executives typically call meetings, start negotiations, and hire consultants and lawyers. Although these steps can be helpful, they can prove disappointing unless executives have taken the time, and the necessary steps, to carve out a powerful position for themselves in the debate. From a position of strength, leaders can bring forth their vision of what is right in a situation; from a position of weakness, leaders' actions are hollow and desperate. Also, before CEOs can step forth onto society's broad stage with a personal vision, they must make sure that their actions will not jeopardize the well-being of their companies, the jobs of employees, and the net income of shareholders. That means asking, *Have I done all I can to secure my position and the strength and stability of my organization?*

In 1988, Eduoard Sakiz, CEO of Roussel Uclaf, a French pharmaceutical company, faced a defining moment of this magnitude. Sakiz had to decide whether to market the new drug RU-486, which later came to be known as the French abortion pill. Early tests had shown that the drug was 90% to 95% effective in inducing miscarriages during the first five weeks of a woman's pregnancy. As he considered whether to introduce the drug, Sakiz found himself embroiled in a major international controversy. Antiabortion groups were outraged that the drug was even under consideration. Pro-choice groups believed the drug represented a major step forward in the battle to secure a woman's right to an abortion. Shareholders of Roussel Uclaf's parent company, Hoechst, were for the most part opposed to RU-486's introduction because there had been serious threats of a major boycott against Hoechst if the drug were introduced. To the French government, also a part owner of Roussel Uclaf, RU-486 meant a step forward in its attempts to cut back on back-alley abortions.

There is little doubt that at one level, the decision Sakiz faced was a personal defining moment. He was a physician with a long-standing commitment to RU-486. Earlier in his career while working as a medical researcher, Sakiz had helped develop the chemical compound that the drug was based on. He believed strongly that the drug could help thousands of women, particularly those in poor countries, avoid injury or death from botched abortions. Because he doubted that the drug would make it to market if he were not running the company, Sakiz knew he would have to secure his own position.

At another level, Sakiz had a responsibility to protect the jobs and security of his employees. He understood this to mean taking whatever steps he could to avoid painful boycotts and the risk of violence against the company. His decision was complicated by the fact that some employees were passionately committed to RU-486, whereas others opposed the drug on ethical grounds or feared that the protests and boycotts would harm Roussel Uclaf and its other products.

How could Sakiz protect his own interests and those of his employees and still introduce the drug? Whatever path he chose, he could see that he would have to assume a low public profile. It would be foolish to play the courageous lion and charge forth pronouncing the moral necessity of RU-486. There were simply too many opponents for that approach to work. It could cost him his job and drag the company through a lengthy, painful process of dangerous turmoil.

Astute executives can use defining moments as an opportunity to redefine their company's role in society.

THE ROLE OF THE ORGANIZATION IN SOCIETY

What makes this third type of defining moment so difficult is that executives are asked to form, reveal, and test not only themselves and their work groups but also their entire company and its role in society. That requires forging a plan of action that functions at three levels: the individual, the work group, and society at large. In which areas do we want to lead? In which areas do we want to follow? How should we interact with the government? With shareholders? Leaders must ask themselves, *Have I thought creatively, boldly, and imaginatively about my organization's role in society and its relationship to its stakeholders?*

What role did Sakiz want Roussel Uclaf to play? He certainly did not want to take the easy way out. Sakiz could have pleased his boss in Germany and avoided years of controversy and boycotts by withdrawing entirely from the market for contraceptives and other reproductive drugs. (Nearly all U.S. drug companies have adopted that approach.) Sakiz could have defined Roussel Uclaf's social role in standard terms—as the property of its shareholders—and argued that RU-486 had to be shelved because boycotts against Roussel Uclaf and Hoechst were likely to cost far more than the drug would earn.

Instead, Sakiz wanted to define Roussel Uclaf's role in a daring way: women seeking nonsurgical abortions and their physicians would be among the company's core stakeholders, and the company would support this constituency through astute political activism. That approach resonated with Sakiz's own core values and with what he thought the majority of employees and other stakeholders wanted. It was clear to him that he needed to find a way to introduce the drug onto the market. The only question was how.

FROM VISION TO REALITY

To make their ethical visions a reality, top-level executives must assess their opponents and allies very carefully. What allies do I have inside and outside my company? Which parties will resist or fight my efforts? Have I underestimated their power and tactical skill or overestimated their ethical commitment? Whom will I alienate with my decision? Which parties will retaliate and how? These tactical concerns can be summed up in the question, *What combination of shrewdness, creativity, and tenacity will make my vision a reality?* Machiavelli put it more succinctly: "Should I play the lion or the fox?"

Although we may never know exactly what went through Sakiz's mind, we can infer from his actions that he had no interest in playing the lion. On October 21, 1988, a month after the French government approved RU-486, Sakiz and the executive committee of Roussel Uclaf made their decision. The *New York Times* described the events in this way: "At an October 21 meeting, Sakiz surprised members of the management committee by calling for a discussion of RU-486. There, in Roussel Uclaf's ultramodern boardroom, the pill's long-standing opponents repeated their objections: RU-486 could spark a painful boycott, it was hurting employee morale, management was devoting too much of its time to this controversy. Finally, it would never be hugely profitable because much would be sold on a cost basis to the Third World. After two hours, Sakiz again stunned the committee by calling for a vote. When he raised his own hand in favor of suspending distribution of RU-486, it was clear that the pill was doomed."

The company informed its employees of the decision on October 25. The next day, Roussel Uclaf announced publicly that it was suspending distribution of the drug because of pressure from antiabortion groups. A Roussel Uclaf official explained the decision: "The pressure groups in the United States are very powerful, maybe even more so than in France."

The company's decision and Sakiz's role in it sparked astonishment and anger. The company and its leadership, critics charged, had doomed a promising public-health tool and had set an example of cowardice. Sakiz's colleague and friend, Etienne-Emile Baulieu, whose research had been crucial to developing RU-486, called the decision "morally scandalous" and accused Sakiz of caving in to pressure. Women's groups, family-planning advocates, and physicians in the United States and Europe came down hard on Sakiz's decision. Other critics suggested sarcastically that the company's decision was no surprise because Roussel Uclaf had decided not to produce contraceptive pills in the face of controversy during the 1960s.

Three days after Roussel Uclaf announced that it would suspend distribution, the French minister of health summoned the company's vice chairman to his office and said that if the company did not resume distribution, the government would transfer the patent to another company that would. After the meeting with the minister of health, Roussel Uclaf again stunned the public: it announced the reversal of its initial decision. The company would distribute RU-486 after all.

Sakiz had achieved his goals but in a foxlike manner. He had called out to his allies and rallied them to his side, but had done so in an indirect and shrewd way. He had used the predictable responses of the many stakeholders to orchestrate a series of events that helped achieve his ends, without looking like he was leading the way. In fact, it appeared as if he were giving in to outside pressure.

Sakiz had put into place the three principal components of the third type of defining moment. First, he had secured his own future at the company. The French health ministry, which supported Sakiz, might well have been aggravated if Hoechst had appointed another CEO in Sakiz's place; it could then have retaliated against the German company in a number of ways. In addition, by having the French government participate in the decision, Sakiz was able to deflect some of the controversy about introducing the drug away from the company, protecting employees and the bottom line. Finally, Sakiz had put Roussel Uclaf in a role of technological and social leadership within French, and even international, circles.

A Bow with Great Tension

As we have moved from Steve Lewis to Peter Adario to Eduoard Sakiz, we have progressed through increasingly complex, but similar, challenges. These managers engaged in difficult acts of self-inquiry that led them to take calculated action based on their personal understanding of what was right in the given situation.

But the three met with varying degrees of success. Steve Lewis was able to balance his personal values and the realities of the business world. The result was ethically informed action that advanced his career. Peter Adario had a sound understanding of his personal values but failed to adapt them to the realities he faced in the competitive work environment at Sayer Microworld. As a result, he failed to prevent McNeil's firing and put his own career in peril. Eduoard Sakiz not only stayed closely connected to his personal values and those of his organization but also predicted what his opponents and allies outside the company would do. The result was the introduction of a drug that shook the world.

Defining moments force us to find a balance between our hearts in all their idealism and our jobs in all their messy reality.

The nineteenth-century German philosopher Friedrich Nietzsche once wrote, "I believe it is precisely through the presence of opposites and the feelings they occasion that the great man—the bow with great tension—develops." Defining moments bring those "opposites" and "feelings" together into vivid focus. They force us to find a balance between our hearts in all their idealism and our jobs in all their messy reality. Defining moments then are not merely intellectual exercises; they are opportunities for inspired action and personal growth.

Notes

1. The names in the accounts of Steve Lewis and Peter Adario have been changed to protect the privacy of the principals involved.

Originally published in March–April 1998
Reprint 98201

The Parable of the Sadhu

BOWEN H. MCCOY

Executive Summary

WHEN DOES A GROUP have responsibility for the well-
being of an individual? And what are the differences
between the ethics of the individual and the ethics of the
corporation? Those are the questions Bowen McCoy
wanted readers to explore in this HBR Classic, first published in September–October 1983.

In 1982, McCoy spent several months hiking through
Nepal. Midway through the difficult trek, as he and several others were preparing to attain the highest point of
their climb, they encountered the body of an Indian holy
man, or sadhu. Wearing little clothing and shivering in
the bitter cold, he was barely alive.

McCoy and the other travelers—who included individuals from Japan, New Zealand, and Switzerland, as
well as local Nepali guides and porters—immediately
wrapped him in warm clothing and gave him food and

drink. A few members of the group broke off to help move the sadhu down toward a village two days' journey away, but they soon left him in order to continue their way up the slope.

What happened to the sadhu? In his retrospective commentary, McCoy notes that he never learned the answer to that question. Instead, the sadhu's story only raises more questions. On the Himalayan slope, a collection of individuals was unprepared for a sudden dilemma. They all "did their bit," but the group was not organized enough to take ultimate responsibility for a life. How, asks McCoy in a broader context, do we prepare our organizations and institutions so they will respond appropriately to ethical crises?

LAST YEAR, AS THE FIRST participant in the new six-month sabbatical program that Morgan Stanley has adopted, I enjoyed a rare opportunity to collect my thoughts as well as do some traveling. I spent the first three months in Nepal, walking 600 miles through 200 villages in the Himalayas and climbing some 120,000 vertical feet. My sole Western companion on the trip was an anthropologist who shed light on the cultural patterns of the villages that we passed through.

During the Nepal hike, something occurred that has had a powerful impact on my thinking about corporate ethics. Although some might argue that the experience has no relevance to business, it was a situation in which a basic ethical dilemma suddenly intruded into the lives of a group of individuals. How the group responded holds a lesson for all organizations, no matter how defined.

The Sadhu

The Nepal experience was more rugged than I had anticipated. Most commercial treks last two or three weeks and cover a quarter of the distance we traveled.

My friend Stephen, the anthropologist, and I were halfway through the 60-day Himalayan part of the trip when we reached the high point, an 18,000-foot pass over a crest that we'd have to traverse to reach the village of Muklinath, an ancient holy place for pilgrims.

Six years earlier, I had suffered pulmonary edema, an acute form of altitude sickness, at 16,500 feet in the vicinity of Everest base camp—so we were understandably concerned about what would happen at 18,000 feet. Moreover, the Himalayas were having their wettest spring in 20 years; hip-deep powder and ice had already driven us off one ridge. If we failed to cross the pass, I feared that the last half of our once-in-a-lifetime trip would be ruined.

The night before we would try the pass, we camped in a hut at 14,500 feet. In the photos taken at that camp, my face appears wan. The last village we'd passed through was a sturdy two-day walk below us, and I was tired.

During the late afternoon, four backpackers from New Zealand joined us, and we spent most of the night awake, anticipating the climb. Below, we could see the fires of two other parties, which turned out to be two Swiss couples and a Japanese hiking club.

To get over the steep part of the climb before the sun melted the steps cut in the ice, we departed at 3:30 a.m. The New Zealanders left first, followed by Stephen and myself, our porters and Sherpas, and then the Swiss. The Japanese lingered in their camp. The sky was clear, and we were confident that no spring storm would erupt that day to close the pass.

At 15,500 feet, it looked to me as if Stephen were shuffling and staggering a bit, which are symptoms of altitude sickness. (The initial stage of altitude sickness brings a headache and nausea. As the condition worsens, a climber may encounter difficult breathing, disorientation, aphasia, and paralysis.) I felt strong—my adrenaline was flowing—but I was very concerned about my ultimate ability to get across. A couple of our porters were also suffering from the height, and Pasang, our Sherpa sirdar (leader), was worried.

Just after daybreak, while we rested at 15,500 feet, one of the New Zealanders, who had gone ahead, came staggering down toward us with a body slung across his shoulders. He dumped the almost naked, barefoot body of an Indian holy man—a sadhu—at my feet. He had found the pilgrim lying on the ice, shivering and suffering from hypothermia. I cradled the sadhu's head and laid him out on the rocks. The New Zealander was angry. He wanted to get across the pass before the bright sun melted the snow. He said, "Look, I've done what I can. You have porters and Sherpa guides. You care for him. We're going on!" He turned and went back up the mountain to join his friends.

I took a carotid pulse and found that the sadhu was still alive. We figured he had probably visited the holy shrines at Muklinath and was on his way home. It was fruitless to question why he had chosen this desperately high route instead of the safe, heavily traveled caravan route through the Kali Gandaki gorge. Or why he was shoeless and almost naked, or how long he had been lying in the pass. The answers weren't going to solve our problem.

Stephen and the four Swiss began stripping off their outer clothing and opening their packs. The sadhu was soon clothed from head to foot. He was not able to walk, but he was very much alive. I looked down the mountain and spotted the Japanese climbers, marching up with a horse.

Without a great deal of thought, I told Stephen and Pasang that I was concerned about withstanding the heights to come and wanted to get over the pass. I took off after several of our porters who had gone ahead.

On the steep part of the ascent where, if the ice steps had given way, I would have slid down about 3,000 feet, I felt vertigo. I stopped for a breather, allowing the Swiss to catch up with me. I inquired about the sadhu and Stephen. They said that the sadhu was fine and that Stephen was just behind them. I set off again for the summit.

Stephen arrived at the summit an hour after I did. Still exhilarated by victory, I ran down the slope to congratulate him. He was suffering from altitude sickness—walking 15 steps, then stopping, walking 15 steps, then stopping. Pasang accompanied him all the way up. When I reached

When I reached them, Stephen glared at me and said, "How do you feel about contributing to the death of a fellow man?"

them, Stephen glared at me and said: "How do you feel about contributing to the death of a fellow man?"

I did not completely comprehend what he meant. "Is the sadhu dead?" I inquired.

"No," replied Stephen, "but he surely will be!"

After I had gone, followed not long after by the Swiss, Stephen had remained with the sadhu. When the Japanese had arrived, Stephen had asked to use their horse to transport the sadhu down to the hut. They had refused. He had then asked Pasang to have a group of our porters carry the sadhu. Pasang had resisted the idea, saying that the porters would have to exert all their energy to get themselves over the pass. He believed they could not carry a man down 1,000 feet to the hut, reclimb the slope, and get across safely before the snow melted. Pasang had pressed Stephen not to delay any longer.

The Sherpas had carried the sadhu down to a rock in the sun at about 15,000 feet and pointed out the hut another 500 feet below. The Japanese had given him food and drink. When they had last seen him, he was listlessly throwing rocks at the Japanese party's dog, which had frightened him.

We do not know if the sadhu lived or died.

For many of the following days and evenings, Stephen and I discussed and debated our behavior toward the sadhu. Stephen is a committed Quaker with deep moral vision. He said, "I feel that what happened with the sadhu is a good example of the breakdown between the individual ethic and the corporate ethic. No one person was willing to assume ultimate responsibility for the sadhu. Each was willing to do his bit just so long as it was not too inconvenient. When it got to be a bother, every-one just passed the buck to someone else and took off. Jesus was relevant to a more individualistic stage of soci-ety, but how do we interpret his teaching today in a world filled with large, impersonal organizations and groups?"

I defended the larger group, saying, "Look, we all cared. We all gave aid and comfort. Everyone did his bit. The New Zealander carried him down below the snow line. I took his pulse and suggested we treat him for hypothermia. You and the Swiss gave him clothing and got him warmed up. The Japanese gave him food and water. The Sherpas carried him down to the sun and pointed out the easy trail toward the hut. He was well enough to throw rocks at a dog. What more could we do?"

"You have just described the typical affluent Westerner's response to a problem. Throwing money—in this case, food and sweaters—at it, but not solving the fundamentals!" Stephen retorted.

"What would satisfy you?" I said. "Here we are, a group of New Zealanders, Swiss, Americans, and Japanese who have never met before and who are at the apex of one of the most powerful experiences of our lives. Some years the pass is

I asked "Where is the limit of our responsibility in a situation like this?"

so bad no one gets over it. What right does an almost naked pilgrim who chooses the wrong trail have to disrupt our lives? Even the Sherpas had no interest in risking the trip to help him beyond a certain point."

Stephen calmly rebutted, "I wonder what the Sherpas would have done if the sadhu had been a well-dressed Nepali, or what the Japanese would have done if the sadhu had been a well-dressed Asian, or what you would have done, Buzz, if the sadhu had been a well-dressed Western woman?"

"Where, in your opinion," I asked, "is the limit of our responsibility in a situation like this? We had our own well-being to worry about. Our Sherpa guides were unwilling to jeopardize us or the porters for the sadhu. No one else on the mountain was willing to commit himself beyond certain self-imposed limits."

Stephen said, "As individual Christians or people with a Western ethical tradition, we can fulfill our obligations in such a situation only if one, the sadhu dies in our care; two, the sadhu demonstrates to us that he can undertake the two-day walk down to the village; or three, we carry the sadhu for two days down to the village and persuade someone there to care for him."

"Leaving the sadhu in the sun with food and clothing—where he demonstrated hand-eye coordination by throwing a rock at a dog—comes close to fulfilling items one and two," I answered. "And it wouldn't have made sense to take him to the village where the people appeared to be far less caring than the Sherpas, so the third condition is impractical. Are you really saying that, no matter what the implications, we should, at the drop of a hat, have changed our entire plan?"

The Individual Versus the Group Ethic

Despite my arguments, I felt and continue to feel guilt about the sadhu. I had literally walked through a classic moral dilemma without fully thinking through the consequences. My excuses for my actions include a high adrenaline flow, a superordinate goal, and a once-in-a-lifetime opportunity—common factors in corporate situations, especially stressful ones.

Real moral dilemmas are ambiguous, and many of us hike right through them, unaware that they exist. When, usually after the fact, someone makes an issue of one, we tend to resent his or her bringing it up. Often, when the full import of what we have done (or not done) hits us, we dig into a defensive position from which it is very difficult to emerge. In rare circumstances, we may contemplate what we have done from inside a prison.

Had we mountaineers been free of stress caused by the effort and the high altitude, we might have treated the sadhu differently. Yet isn't stress the real test of personal and corporate values? The instant decisions that executives make under pressure reveal the most about personal and corporate character.

Among the many questions that occur to me when I ponder my experience with the sadhu are: What are the practical limits of moral imagination and vision? Is there a collective or institutional ethic that differs from the ethics of the individual? At what level of effort or commitment can one discharge one's ethical responsibilities?

Not every ethical dilemma has a right solution. Reasonable people often disagree; otherwise there would be no dilemma. In a business context, however, it is essential that managers agree on a process for dealing with dilemmas.

Our experience with the sadhu offers an interesting parallel to business situations. An immediate response was mandatory. Failure to act was a decision in itself. Up on the mountain we could not resign and submit our résumés to a headhunter. In contrast to philosophy, business involves action and implementation— getting things done. Managers must come up with answers based on what they see and what they allow to influence their decision-making processes. On the mountain, none of us but Stephen realized the true dimensions of the situation we were facing.

As a group, we had no process for developing a consensus. We had no sense of purpose or plan.

One of our problems was that as a group we had no process for developing a consensus. We had no sense of purpose or plan. The difficulties of dealing with the sadhu were so complex that no one person could handle them. Because the group did not have a set of

preconditions that could guide its action to an acceptable resolution, we reacted instinctively as individuals.
The cross-cultural nature of the group added a further
layer of complexity. We had no leader with whom we
could all identify and in whose purpose we believed. Only
Stephen was willing to take charge, but he could not gain
adequate support from the group to care for the sadhu.

Some organizations do have values that transcend the
personal values of their managers. Such values, which go
beyond profitability, are usually revealed when the organization is under stress. People throughout the organization generally accept its values, which, because they are
not presented as a rigid list of commandments, may be
somewhat ambiguous. The stories people tell, rather
than printed materials, transmit the organization's con-
ceptions of what is proper behavior.

For 20 years, I have been exposed at senior levels to a
variety of corporations and organizations. It is amazing
how quickly an outsider can sense the tone and style of
an organization and, with that, the degree of tolerated
openness and freedom to challenge management.

Organizations that do not have a heritage of mutually
accepted, shared values tend to become unhinged during
stress, with each individual bailing out for himself or her-
self. In the great takeover battles we have witnessed during past years, companies that had strong cultures drew
the wagons around them and fought it out, while other
companies saw executives—supported by golden
parachutes—bail out of the struggles.

Because corporations and their members are interde-
pendent, for the corporation to be strong the members
need to share a preconceived notion of correct behavior,
a "business ethic," and think of it as a positive force, not
a constraint.

As an investment banker, I am continually warned by well-meaning lawyers, clients, and associates to be wary of conflicts of interest. Yet if I were to run away from every difficult situation, I wouldn't be an effective investment banker. I have to feel my way through conflicts. An effective manager can't run from risk either; he or she has to confront risk. To feel "safe" in doing that, managers need the guidelines of an agreed-upon process and set of values within the organization.

After my three months in Nepal, I spent three months as an executive-in-residence at both the Stanford Business School and the University of California at Berkeley's Center for Ethics and Social Policy of the Graduate Theological Union. Those six months away from my job gave me time to assimilate 20 years of business experience. My thoughts turned often to the meaning of the leadership role in any large organization. Students at the seminary thought of themselves as antibusiness. But when I questioned them, they agreed that they distrusted all large organizations, including the church. They perceived all large organizations as impersonal and opposed to individual values and needs. Yet we all know of organizations in which people's values and beliefs are respected and their expressions encouraged. What makes the difference? Can we identify the difference and, as a result, manage more effectively?

The word *ethics* turns off many and confuses more. Yet the notions of shared values and an agreed-upon process for dealing with adversity and change—what many people mean when they talk about corporate culture—seem to be at the heart of the ethical issue. People who are in touch with their own core beliefs and the beliefs of others and who are sustained by them can be more comfortable living on the cutting edge. At times,

taking a tough line or a decisive stand in a muddle of
ambiguity is the only ethical thing to do. If a manager is
indecisive about a problem and spends time trying to
figure out the "good" thing to do, the enterprise may
be lost.

Business ethics, then, has to do with the authenticity
and integrity of the enterprise. To be ethical is to follow
the business as well as the cultural goals of the corporation, its owners, its employees, and its customers. Those
who cannot serve the corporate vision are not authentic
businesspeople and, therefore, are not ethical in the
business sense.

At this stage of my own business experience, I have a
strong interest in organizational behavior. Sociologists
are keenly studying what they call corporate stories, leg-
ends, and heroes as a way organizations have of trans-
mitting value systems. Corporations such as Arco have
even hired consultants to perform an audit of their corporate culture. In a company, a leader is a person who
understands, interprets, and manages the corporate
value system. Effective managers, therefore, are action-
oriented people who resolve conflict, are tolerant of
ambiguity, stress, and change, and have a strong sense of
purpose for themselves and their organizations.

If all this is true, I wonder about the role of the professional manager who moves from company to company.
How can he or she quickly absorb the values and culture
of different organizations? Or is there, indeed, an art of
management that is totally transportable? Assuming
that such fungible managers do exist, is it proper for
them to manipulate the values of others?

What would have happened had Stephen and I carried the sadhu for two days back to the village and
become involved with the villagers in his care? In four

trips to Nepal, my most interesting experience occurred in 1975 when I lived in a Sherpa home in the Khumbu for five days while recovering from altitude sickness. The high point of Stephen's trip was an invitation to participate in a family funeral ceremony in Manang. Neither experience had to do with climbing the high passes of the Himalayas. Why were we so reluctant to try the lower path, the ambiguous trail? Perhaps because we did not have a leader who could reveal the greater purpose of the trip to us.

Why didn't Stephen, with his moral vision, opt to take the sadhu under his personal care? The answer is partly because Stephen was hard-stressed physically himself and partly because, without some support system that encompassed our involuntary and episodic community on the mountain, it was beyond his individual capacity to do so.

I see the current interest in corporate culture and corporate value systems as a positive response to pessimism such as Stephen's about the decline of the role of the individual in large organizations. Individuals who operate from a thoughtful set of personal values provide the foundation for a corporate culture. A corporate tradition that encourages freedom of inquiry, supports personal values, and reinforces a focused sense of direction can fulfill the need to combine individuality with the prosperity and success of the group. Without such corporate support, the individual is lost.

That is the lesson of the sadhu. In a complex corporate situation, the individual requires and deserves the support of the group. When people cannot find such support in their organizations, they don't know how to act. If such support is forthcoming, a person has a stake in the success of the group and can add much to the process of establishing and maintaining a corporate culture. Management's challenge is to be sensitive to individual needs, to shape them, and to direct and focus them for the benefit of the group as a whole.

For each of us the sadhu lives. Should we stop what we are doing and comfort him; or should we keep trudging up toward the high pass? Should I pause to help the derelict I pass on the street each night as I walk by the Yale Club en route to Grand Central Station? Am I his brother? What is the nature of our responsibility if we consider ourselves to be ethical persons? Perhaps it is to change the values of the group so that it can, with all its resources, take the other road.

When Do We Take a Stand?

I WROTE ABOUT MY experiences purposely to present an ambiguous situation. I never found out if the sadhu lived or died. I can attest, though, that the sadhu lives on in his story. He lives in the ethics classes I teach each year at business schools and churches. He lives in the classrooms of numerous business schools, where professors have taught the case to tens of thousands of students. He lives in several casebooks on ethics and on an educational video. And he lives in organizations such as the American Red Cross and AT&T, which use his story in their ethics training.

As I reflect on the sadhu now, 15 years after the fact, I first have to wonder, What actually happened on that Himalayan slope? When I first wrote about the event, I reported the experience in as much detail as I could remember, but I shaped it to the needs of a good classroom discussion. After years of reading my story, viewing it on video, and hearing others discuss it, I'm not sure I myself know what actually occurred on the mountainside that day!

I've also heard a wide variety of responses to the story. The sadhu, for example, may not have wanted our help at all—he may have been intentionally bringing on his own death as a way to holiness. Why had he taken the dangerous way over the pass instead of the caravan route through the gorge? Hindu businesspeople have told me that in trying to assist the sadhu, we were being typically arrogant Westerners imposing our cultural values on the world.

I've learned that each year along the pass, a few Nepali porters are left to freeze to death outside the tents of the unthinking tourists who hired them. A few years ago, a French group even left one of their own, a young French woman, to die there. The difficult pass seems to demonstrate a perverse version of Gresham's law of currency: The bad practices of previous travelers have driven out the values that new travelers might have followed if they were at home. Perhaps that helps to explain why our porters behaved as they did and why it was so difficult for Stephen or anyone else to establish a different approach on the spot.

Our Sherpa sirdar, Pasang, was focused on his responsibility for bringing us up the mountain safe and sound. (His livelihood and status in the Sherpa ethnic group depended on our safe return.) We were weak, our party was split, the porters were well on their way to the top with all our gear and food, and a storm would have separated us irrevocably from our logistical base.

The fact was, we had no plan for dealing with the contingency of the sadhu. There was nothing we could do to unite our multicultural group in the little time we had. An ethical dilemma had come upon us unexpectedly, an element of drama that may explain why the sadhu's story has continued to attract students.

I am often asked for help in teaching the story. I usually advise keeping the details as ambiguous as possible. A true ethical dilemma requires a decision between two hard choices. In the case of the sadhu, we had to decide how much to sacrifice ourselves to take care of a stranger. And given the constraints of our trek, we had to make a group decision, not an individual one. If a large majority of students in a class ends up thinking I'm a bad person because of my decision on the mountain, the instructor may not have given the case its due. The same is true if the majority sees no problem with the choices we made.

Any class's response depends on its setting, whether it's a business school, a church, or a corporation. I've found that younger students are more likely to see the issue as black-and-white, whereas older ones tend to see shades of gray. Some have seen a conflict between the different ethical approaches that we followed at the time. Stephen felt he had to do everything he could to save the sadhu's life, in accordance with his Christian ethic of compassion. I had a utilitarian response: do the greatest good for the greatest number. Give a burst of aid to minimize the sadhu's exposure, then continue on our way.

The basic question of the case remains, When do we take a stand? When do we allow a "sadhu" to intrude into our daily lives? Few of us can afford the time or effort to take care of every needy person we encounter. How much must we give of ourselves? And how do we prepare our organizations and institutions so they will respond appropriately in a crisis? How do we influence them if we do not agree with their points of view?

We cannot quit our jobs over every ethical dilemma, but if we continually ignore our sense of values, who do we become? As a journalist asked at a recent conference on ethics, "Which ditch are we willing to die in?" For each of us, the answer is a bit different. How we act in response to that question defines better than anything else who we are, just as, in a collective sense, our acts define our institutions. In effect, the sadhu is always there, ready to remind us of the tensions between our own goals and the claims of strangers.

Originally published in May–June 1997
Reprint 97307

About the Contributors

At the time this article was originally published, KENNETH R. ANDREWS was the Donald K. David Professor of Business Administration, Emeritus, at the Harvard Business School. He was editor of the *Harvard Business Review* from 1979 to 1985. This article is adapted from his introduction to *Ethics in Practice: Managing the Moral Corporation* (HBS Press, 1989).

JOSEPH L. BADARACCO, JR., is the John Shad Professor of Business Ethics at Harvard Business School. He teaches courses on strategy, general management, and business ethics in the School's M.B.A. and executive programs. Badaracco is a graduate of St. Louis University, Oxford University, where he was a Rhodes Scholar, and Harvard Business School, where he earned an M.B.A. and a D.B.A. Badaracco is also Faculty Chair for the M.B.A. Elective Curriculum and the past chairman of the Harvard University Advisory Committee on Shareholder Responsibility. Professor Badaracco has taught in executive programs in the United States, Japan, and several other countries. He is a director of Excelon Corporation and faculty chair of the Nomura School of Advanced Management in Tokyo. He is the author of *Loading the Dice, Leadership and the Quest for Integrity, The Knowledge Link, Business Ethics: Roles and Responsibilities,* and *Defining Moments: When Managers Must Choose between Right and Right.* These books have been translated into nine languages. His latest book, published in

February 2002, is *Leading Quietly: An Unorthodox Guide to Doing the Right Thing.*

At the time this article was originally published, THOMAS DONALDSON was a professor at the Wharton School of the University of Pennsylvania in Philadelphia, where he taught business ethics. He wrote *The Ethics of International Business* (Oxford University Press, 1989) and is the coauthor, with Thomas W. Dunfee, of *Ties That Bind: A Social Contracts Approach to Business Ethics* (HBS Press, 1999).

At the time this article was originally published, SAUL W. GELLERMAN was the dean of the University of Dallas Graduate School of Management. He is the author of eight books on management and of the *Harvard Business Review* article "Supervision: Substance and Style" (March–April 1976).

At the time this article was originally published, BOWEN H. MCCOY was a real estate and business counselor, a teacher, and a philanthropist. He retired from Morgan Stanley in 1990 after twenty-eight years of service.

LAURA L. NASH is Senior Research Fellow at Harvard Business School and founding partner of Piper Cove Asset Management LLC. For the past twenty years she has taught and written on values and leadership and has authored or coauthored seven books. She is currently writing a book with Professor Howard Stevenson on enduring success.

LYNN SHARP PAINE is John G. McLean Professor of Business Administration at the Harvard Business School and author of *Value Shift: Why Companies Must Merge Social and Financial Imperatives to Achieve Superior Performance* (McGraw-Hill, 2003). She was a member of the Conference Board's Blue Ribbon Commission on Public Trust and Private Enterprise, whose recommendations for corporate governance in the post-Enron era were issued in January 2003.

Index